WHY ENTREPRENEURSHIP?

SDF	JPN	BNT	ABN	TTL
2.22	0.77	5.32	4.40	2.78

What is IT All About?
Part 1

Why Entrepreneurship?

What is IT All About?

By

FREDERIQUE MEDIA PRODUCTIONS

Edited by

Charlotte Evans, PhD

Suzanne Sophia Frederique

http://whyentrepreneurship.com

http://fmp.frederiquecapital.com

http://facebook.com/whyentrepreneurship

Published by

FREDERIQUE Media Productions

Second Edition: March 2014

Copyright © 2014 Frederique Media Productions

Paperback
ISBN-10:0988339129
ISBN-13:978-0-9883391-2-5

EBook
ISBN-10: 0988339137
ISBN-13: 978-0-9883391-3-2

This book was printed in the United States of America.

PREFACE

I remember the day so well. It was a typical Saturday evening and my wife and I were heading home for the night. We had only been married a few weeks at the time, I think. We decided to stop by our local ice cream store, as we often do, only that day, we were having a very interesting conversation about life. As I pulled up to the ice cream store and parked the car, my wife made the most profound statement of her life. She said, "I feel like is this it for my life. I come home and go to work each day and repeat the same process all over again, day in day out. I do the same things at work. It feels like our lives are supposed to be just work, have children, getting old, and die."

My wife, at the time, sounded like the average employee-minded person. She was trapped by the monotony of life and work. She felt as if she had no purpose. If anything, her job was her life's purpose. Like many of her colleagues, she had worked the same job for over ten years when I met her. All she did was come home and watch her soap operas for the night, call it a day after a quiet TV dinner. That was her usual routine.

Unlike my wife, I had spent the last ten years or so working on becoming an entrepreneur. Hoping to one day be able to walk away from my day time job and pursue entrepreneurship fulltime, I had just walked away from a successful business venture and was looking for the next thing to get involved in. I had already spent my whole life understanding and reflecting on my life's purpose and what I believed God wanted me to do with my life. I had also been a student of personal development since 2001.

When she started asking about purpose and work, I began explaining my answer to her in terms of business. It was all that I knew that made sense to me.

After we got the ice cream, she was mad at me because I had related everything back to entrepreneurship. She really did not understand where I was coming from and she probably didn't think I was listening to her. It was one of those conversations where my wife wanted me to listen and not speak. The five minute drive home had us fighting for hours.

"Not everything is about business," She insisted, which is the statement that led to the biggest argument of our marriage on November, 2008. It would also be the game changer that led me to writing this book. It was clear my wife did not really know me. She did not understand what I stood for and that I was a man destined for greatness. I had a vision for my family. Apparently my wife really did not take me seriously. She did not understand that I wanted more for my life and my family; that I understood my purpose and I had a clear vision of what was to come in the near future. This was the reason why I was working hard on becoming an entrepreneur. So I could protect my family for what was to come. To me, entrepreneurship explains everything that is and must be done to prepare for the economic war ahead of us.

What angered me most, that afternoon, was my wife's inability to understand the importance of what I was working on, or even to consider it.

As a newlywed, I felt like I had just made the biggest mistake of my life marrying someone who did not share the same vision I had for myself and my family. I thought she would undermine every plan, every stride that I was embarking on to free our family from the enslavement of what I saw as a representation of just over broke (JOB) mentality.

I was at a loss for words that I didn't speak to my wife for a whole week. I really did not know what to do. To work hard in building a legacy and not have your partner involved was pointless; it seemed totally pointless. I will explain this in part 2.

It took me a week of deep reflection and prayer to figure out how I could go about helping my wife understand what I was trying to do and how everything actually has to do with business. I found the answer, though, in the most unlikely place – my wife's soap operas.

As I had stated earlier, my wife would spend her evenings catching up on her favorite soap operas through Soap Net on the cable network. One day, I happened to be paying attention to one of these shows - *General Hospital, All My Children, Young & the Restless*. And to be honest with you, as a kid, I remember watching some of those shows with my mother and aunt. That was what most of their conversations were about, too, when I was a kid. They lived and breathe these addictive shows.

Nevertheless, it did not take long for me to realize the obvious. Every single one of those soaps were based on the life of the wealthy. Everyone had a business or was related in some way to someone else that had a business. The businesses of these characters, their entrepreneurial focus, allowed them the freedom to roam around yapping to each other. I really thought that was the funniest thing ever. I was actually so intrigued by these characters that I started watching one of the shows to confirm this. And it was true. Who in their right mind could sit at a job, talk personal business all day, have affairs, and other dramas that are typical of soap operas, all while actually holding on to a job? How could these people not get fired? That world does not exist!

And here was my wife talking about "not everything has to do with business" as she stared at a TV screen every night, watching the glamorous life of wealthy business men and women; people drinking the finest wines, eating at the finest sports clubs, living in the most lavish mansions with maids. Yet she ponders at the question, "I feel like, is this it for my life?"

The answer was right in front of her all this time. I was shocked and amazed by what I was seeing and listening to; people talking about stock options, buy outs, mergers, and takeovers. In the mist of it all, my wife did not understand the language of the rich. She did not understand, like my mother and others alike, the language that was actually being spoken. I did, as clear as day, but that was not what was so interesting to my mother, aunt, and wife. They were so caught up in the plot and the absurd glamor of everything that they never could imagine how they might actually achieve the same status. If they would just get off the couch and turn off that TV, they too could start pursuing the same life style that they were feeding off of, watching every day, five days a week, and now with TiVo, 24-7.

This realization about the soap operas was the eye opener that changed my life and our marriage. Nevertheless, it took me another year pondering over the details of this book before I took action.

People need to read what I have to say about our future, our legacy, our last hope for freedom. My wife's story made me realized that there were too many people out there like her; who do not understand the significance of the next couple of years; who do not understand that their life is more than a job.

There are too many people who do not understand that their struggle and the hunger inside of them is there for a reason. The talents given to them were put in place by God and for a divine purpose, but rarely are they aware of this.

I don't believe in luck, fate, or whatever else you want to call it. Each of us has a purpose on this Earth. Whether you use your talents for good or bad it is to be determined by you. Sometimes man has to take the road less traveled to find his true self.

When I began planning to write this book, I did not know how much it would change my life, my thinking, and my purpose. Since I was a kid, I believed that each word spoken by me to someone else had significance and a purpose. That is why I don't waste my time talking about nonsense that is not relevant to me or my spiritual growth. I don't waste my words. The power of a wise man is in the tongue. Today I see things much clearer. I have an even closer relationship with God than I ever had before because I am pursuing my purpose for God's kingdom in my life. I hope you can achieve the same level of clarity after reading this book.

In the process of writing this book, it became clear to me that it was more for my validation than necessarily for you, the reader, that I have compiled this book to help explain the importance of preparing for the worst. This book also serves as my attempt to fulfill my own destiny and leave a lasting legacy as well. My struggle, thus far, was God's way of leading me to get to this very point in my life. Always remember that within the words, "history" is your story. Everything is already planned; God is ready for you to finish the race. You just have to get started.

In writing *Why Entrepreneurship? What is IT all about?* I make references to entities like the government, the school system, and corporate America so often that I have decided to refer to them in one word, the "systems." I did this in part because they really are a collaboration of establishments so deeply rooted in American tradition that they cannot be separated. Each one plays a role in keeping you and I enslaved to a job. It is, after all, part of a larger conspiracy, if you want to call it that, to keep us in line with false ideologies and belief systems. From time to time I will specifically refer to one by name but overall, I consider them all under the same umbrella of systems.

Drawing this introduction to a close, however, I would like to make three points. The first one is that this book is really three books in one. First and foremost, this book is about why you need to become an entrepreneur. In each chapter, you will read countless examples for why this is essential for your future. Second, this book is about life; accomplishing your dreams, and finding your purpose for living which is why entrepreneurship is one vehicle that will help you achieve those dreams and goals. Third, this book is about financial literacy and financial freedom. While most of us have some basic understanding of finance, entrepreneurship forces us to dive head first in all aspect that is financially related to our business. Hence the relation to our lives, dreams, goals, and purpose for living.

To truly do it all, we must have a greater understanding of our finances; so we don't end up being enslaved to our debtors or the fiat money we work so hard to possess. *(Proverbs 22:7&1 Corinthians 7:23).* Hence I have taken the liberty of breaking the book into three distinct parts. Part one is on finding your purpose. Part two is on business and network marketing. Part three is about the perseveration of wealth and leaving a legacy behind.

The second point I would like to make is in reference to God throughout the book. I speak of God the Father because that is the Catholic faith and now Christian faith that I practice. I did not write this book to offend anyone's religion or make believe that the Christian faith is the one true religion that should be followed. Since I can only be of one faith, I reference the Lord because that is the only God or religion that I can truly speak of. It is by no means intended to neglect or leave out otherworld religions. It is my hope that when I speak of Jesus Christ, that I speak in recognition of all other religious beliefs. Please feel free to substitute my mention of God, the father for your own religious beliefs such as Islam, Judaism, Catholicism, and Buddhism.

Last but not least, unlike most successful authors you have read in the past, I am not writing this book from the top down but rather from the bottom up. I live, breath, and have experienced it all. There is nothing hyped or exaggerated to express a point. These are my thoughts, philosophies, and vision for the future; what I see as possible base on the track record we are on. These words are backed by various authors, philosophers, and the American people whom I had a chance to watch, speak with, and live alongside in their struggle for survival.

I have been taught by the very best in the industry to leave golden nuggets of wisdom along the way so others can see the light and follow in my footstep to salvation. If there was ever such a wiser man who could have taught me this philosophy, I would have to say it was Bertram L. Calhoun out of Baltimore, Maryland who instilled in me the importance of leaving nuggets of wisdom along the way. For that alone, I am so very grateful.

To follow in his wisdom I placed bread crumbs and golden nuggets of my own throughout this book in the form of italicize books that I have read or referenced. I don't want you to just read my book as face value and say that was a good book. I want you to read the facts for yourself and obtain the same knowledge that I have gained over the years. This way you will never forget the reasons why you have decided to embark into this journey with me. It is my hope you will have learned the reasons why your WHY must be strong in the coming years or why you must renew it or make it even stronger.

These nuggets will be your guide. I may not have all the answers as time changes, but I can sure help you start on your own venture to the promise land of financial freedom. It is my hope you will become stronger and wiser because of it and likewise pass on the knowledge.

Please visit my websites, http://facebook.com/whyentrepreneurship and http://whyentrepreneurship.com. Share your story of what you plan on doing or have already started to do to change your family legacy under the blog section for this book.

This book does not end at the end with its last page. Rather it is only the beginning. This book continues on with your feedback online and on http://Voices4theVoiceless.com. Voices4theVoiceless will forever be an extension of this book online as the global economy changes. However it is my hope to see your words bring inspiration to others on my blog section or see you face to face at a future lecture hall.

In the words of my mentors, "I hope to see you at the top, for the bottom is too crowded."

To Your Success!

Dimitry Frederique

ACKNOWLEDGMENT

When I met my wife, Suzanne S. Frederique I knew it would be the start of something great. I would have never guess that it would take her to spark the passion I have for this book out of me. She is not only my wife but my friend. I am so proud to see her increase her financial intelligence each year. I know one day our children's legacy will be secured through her. Thanks for the inspiration.

I thank God for putting people in our lives for a purpose, a reason, and for a season. Special thanks to those who have been my closest friends over the years: Tanisha Roebuck, Albertha Bogan, Tony Prescott, Linda L. Johnson, Evelyn E. Robinson, Walter J. Norris III, and Angelo Manoloules. My friends have not only been business partners over the years but have become great supporters; they have been through it all with me. For that I thank you all.

To my business associates over the years, colleagues, and mentors – your words, thoughts, wisdom, and struggle for financial freedom are all with me. May this book be a representation of your journey to freedom and spark the true vision for tomorrow's leaders that will soon follow the same path to freedom. As I see, all the warning signs are just a few short years away. I felt this was the right time to put it all together and publish this book. This book was in my heart and spirit for many years before I knew what to do with this information.

I also want to recognize James Chilaka, Barbara A. Dulin, and Mrs. Browne for all their contribution to this book. Their stories were worth telling because they played a vital role in demonstrating the realities we live in today. It is stories like theirs that have encouraged me to continue on with this book when I doubt myself at times if this was a worthy cause.

Special thanks goes to God. You are the Rock that steers my foundation. The words that I am about to share with you all are truly an inspiration from God's vision within me. If God did not give me the gift of foresight to see what is to come, I would have missed it like most of us will. I always believed that I was born with a purpose and a destiny. Thanks be to God for all the guidance thus far and for shaping my life for this point in time.

I also have to thank God for putting rivals and obstacles in front of me; for keeping me uncomfortable at each job. If it was not for them, I still would have been wondering in the desert with a big void in my life.

I want to thank my enemies, my oppressors; those who held me back and never wanted to see me succeed at anything. Your effort to achieve a strong hold on my life has given me strength throughout the years and created a resiliency that will be passed on to my children. Your opposition taught me to never give up or quit. It is these struggles that made me a fighter, that made me yearn for more; to want to leave behind a legacy for my children's children one day.

To all evil doers, thank you all for playing your role in my life. You had a purpose as well and I have come to appreciate the part that you played in trying to hold me down. Unfortunately God sent me with a bigger mission and one that cannot be defeated by mankind. I am the anointed one sent to deliver a message to all who will listen.

I also want to acknowledge all those who come to America in search of hope, freedom, and in search for the land of opportunity. Witnessing your struggles and financial battle to be given some form of dignity at your place of work while barely speaking English is one of the reasons why I needed to tell your story; for the reasons why you too need to become an entrepreneur. Last but not least, I want to give thanks and recognition to my hard working American countrymen. The one true home that I have grown to know and love. Nevertheless if it was not for my birth place of Haiti, I would have never known to love and respect the life that has been given to me by God. So to my hard working American people, I see your strength, your potential for greatness, and the power to create great wealth and overcome major obstacles ahead. I also see your pain, your self-destruction ahead, and your children - the legacy you will leave behind for them.

Unfortunately at times, we are all blind to the mess we have created from within. It is always hard to see the invincible shackles lurking around our knees and arms, to awaken us from imprisonment.

This great nation was built on the backs of slaves and today it continues to be built on the backs of all Americans who dare to ask the government, the systems, what can you do for me?

Sadly enough, the American workforce has yet to realize that the new and improved shackles are called economic enslavement. They cannot be heard or seen. Economic enslavement is a silent killer of your dreams and future.

I pray that those American people have worked long and hard to create this land, your land, will wake up before it is too late to save this generation and the legacy that is your children's future.

May God watch over us all!

LET US PRAY

Dear God,

We have come before you once again, seeking your wisdom and guidance. I know that it is because of your will that I stand before you. I give all the glory and honor to you, my Lord and savior. I know it is through you that all my blessings flow. May you touch and bless the lives of those who will hear your beckon call for change.

Thank you for this glorious opportunity that you have bestowed upon me to fulfill your work. May you open the minds and ears of those who have read this book or listened to the sound of my voice. That you give them all the strength and courage that they need to believe in themselves. That they were created with your purpose in mind from the very beginning of time.

Thank you for opening my eyes to the problems facing our future. For you have brought us back full circle, and we are begging you, on our knees, for hope and prosperity.

Please breathe life once again into our souls so that we can fulfill your divine purpose, as children of the Earth.

Lord, let it be known that it is not my intention to offend anyone who hears the sound of my voice or reads this book. I am only your messenger from God's chosen vessels. I am only here to serve you. May your wisdom glorify your name, oh, Lord, my God. It is only through your will, God, that I stand witness to the miracles you are about to do in the lives of your chosen vessels. My strength is in the hands of God. And if by any chance, what I have said bears a heavy burden upon your heart, please understand that it is God, seeking your attention to change your ways. To seek out a better path for your life and the generation to follow. You have ignored his designed plan for your future far too long. The Lord has been crying out to you, for so long to seek an alternative path, the one less traveled. You don't have to worry or fear that his direction will steer you off course. The Lord wants me to tell you today, for I have seen the beginning and the end. And the end that I have for you is greater than the one you can imagine. So be not afraid of the challenges ahead of you. I will always be right here, with you, throughout the journey. Just listen to my voice and I will guide you through it all, says the Lord. It is my only promise to you. So keep the faith and follow the destiny I have set forth before you. And it is my hope that you will leave here fulfilled with a clear mission for God's glory in your life.

And let all of God's children say,

Amen!

TABLE OF CONTENTS

Part 1
"Once you understand your purpose, your mission on earth becomes clear."

If you have not put any thought into the subject matters in this book or have never considered why it is necessary to leave a legacy for your family, I suggest you begin today. Your children's future will depend on your actions going forward from this point on.

PART 1

"ONCE YOU UNDERSTAND YOUR PURPOSE,
YOUR MISSION ON EARTH BECOMES CLEAR."

CHAPTER 1

What is My Purpose on this Earth?

WHAT IS MY PURPOSE?

I grew up in America, watching *Star Trek, The Next Generation*. It would become one of my favorite shows, leading me to fall in love with science and technology. How fitting, too, that this show would be the starting point for my discourse on living a purposeful life.

For those who have never watched Star Trek, on the show, there was a cybernetic life form called the Borg. They had one mission, one purpose for their existence, which was to assimilate other life forms and bring them into their collective of one species to rule the universe.

Of course, this may sound like a far fetch beginning to a discussion on a subject as serious as seeking out your purpose. Please indulge me, though, because the Borg, like the Replicators from the hit TV series *Stargate SG-1*, have only one goal in life, to assimilate and nothing else.

These alien creatures have a one track mind to replicate themselves into a collective of one. These creatures or fictional characters never deviated from their initial existence or evolution because they only serve one purpose.

No matter how advanced they got, they were all a collective of one mind. They still grew in numbers and had conquered a large amount of territory through expansion yet they never deviated from their goal and mission. They maintained a level of communication throughout the galaxy. They stayed in unison.

Sometimes I wish the human race was more like the Borgs or Replicators so that we can continue to pass on our family mission and heritage to each new generation that is born. This would create a new world order instead of the chaos that we have left for our children. Their one mission in life would be to continue to grow the legacy that was entrusted to them by finding mates who shared in the same vision, mission, and purpose for a new family to be born. The goal would be the same for every family on earth - assimilate knowledge, gain awareness, and understanding through each generation and build on the success from the pass to continue the family name through entrepreneurship.

In fact, I really believe that we will never be ready to explore the universe or leave our own Milky Way or even make contact with other life forms until we have learned to evolve as one species, with a common goal or vision for the human race. If we do not have an identity when we leave our planet or solar system one day, how can we tell other life forms about who we are?

Now, you may think the discussion so far has nothing to do with purpose and business but it has everything to do with the title of this book, *Why Entrepreneurship*? What is IT All About?

Humans, as a collective, are the only species on Earth that do not act with any real kind of unity. We do as we please and evolve over time, without a real consensus of where are we going in each generation. I know for sure that technology, amongst everything else, drives us to evolve. At the same time it does not give us a sense of direction and purpose. We simply make it up as we go along, seeking a better quality of life without really knowing *what is IT all about* in the first place.

When we think about human evolution and life, we hardly put the two together and say, "I am raising my children or I am giving birth, or creating a life for a purpose."

Animals, on the other hand, procreate based on survival instincts and because nature determines when it is the season for them to mate and start a new life. For lack of a better word, it is an evolutionary cycle for which they cannot control the urge while we are the only species that have control of our urges to mate or procreate a new life. Hence we have evolved from being an animal, to being Nomads, and now, as individuals, who can expand and evolve.

Within our evolutionary time line as Apes and now to human beings, we walked away from the collective thinking as one race, one species, or one being. Through time and now in the 21st century, we have evolved to become individuals, free to make our own choices and decisions about life and procreation. Unlike the Borgs and Replicators, who were able to expand across the universe and maintain their collectiveness with one mission, one purpose; we, as human beings, seemed to have done the opposite the more we move away from one another and explored the planet.

I cannot help but be reminded of something powerful that Malcolm Gladswell wrote in his book, *The Tipping Point*. He writes of a special magic number, 150. This number is very important to the human collective because his research shows that after a group of people have reached that number, the collective group or people in that group eventually fall apart. They cannot sustain or maintain the cohesiveness of a family or culture through name recognition or facial recognition that each other is part of that one group or collective. In other words, due to the sheer size of that group beyond 150, people become strangers to one another. There is no more familiarity.

We all can relate to this when we go to family reunions or visit what was once a small family of four children, for example, the children having grown up to have families of their own. Some have two or three kids of their own. Others had more. The pack has grown but is still manageable. When we start counting the new extensions of the family through in-laws though, it starts becoming harder and harder to manage. Knowing who is who by name or face becomes incredibly difficult.

We see that today in our own families. Aside from the basic upbringing that our parents gave us, our children eventually create their own communication skills, purpose, and mission and walked away from what they were taught in their generation. Each generation has reinvented the wheel and separated from the core teachings of faith, family, and mission passed on from parent to parent.

Today we use the words, "old school ideas" and "back in the day" to describe a way of thinking or doing things that is far from modern day. And that is in part to what technology has done to us as we depend on it so much more for survival.

So how do we find meaning in our lives and seek out our purpose when we have drifted from the collective - our parents? There has been a war going on since the invention of the idiot box, a war to win our children over from the mass media or propaganda that is, think and do for yourself.

Today's generation of kids do not see the need to listen to the wisdom of their parents. Even worse, we are living with a generation of young kids that are babies themselves having children at such a young age that they cannot offer any wisdom to their offspring. Teenage mothers are in fact learning directly from their mistakes as they (mother and child) both grow up together and learn from the errors of their ways.

As for adults who were raised in a conservative life style or upbringing, how do you fight the enemy inside that has prevented you from seeking your purpose? You are stuck all your life at a dead end job, avoiding something you actually wanted to do because you had your parents telling you it was not a good career path, your parents or elders did not know how you would be able to support yourself on that kind of salary. Sad to say, later on in life we find ourselves giving the same lectures to our own children.

Would it not be a perfect world if everyone was doing what they love to do and could really be happy doing it? Could you imagine the quality of work that would be performed and the customer satisfaction ratings? Everyone would take their time to appreciate their trade or craft. Our jobs would be an extension of who we are.

As a kid, I dreamt it would be possible to swap out with someone else who was not happy doing what they wanted to do; like a match-making job swap program for adults who are not happy with what they are doing any more.

Unfortunately that is not the reality of the world we live in. Instead we are grumpy, physically there but not really present to interact with our colleagues if you know what I mean. We drag our feet at work, we dread getting up to go to work. We can't wait for the day to be over or our shift to end soon. You get the point.

However long the day may seem, we find ourselves day dreaming of a better tomorrow - living the life that we wish could come true or finally having the courage to quit our job and follow our dreams, our passion in life.

Have you ever asked yourself this question or ever wondered about it? Why do I feel stuck at this dead end job? Better yet, have you asked, is this all that my life was meant for? Even Oprah Winfrey prayed about fulfilling her purpose in life long before she accepted the life time achievement award at the 25th Annual Daytime Emmy Awards in 1998[i].

So what is your purpose for living, breathing, and even existing? Most of us have never taken the time to think about these types of questions. For those of us who have reflected on our lives, it probably feels like we were popped out of our mother's womb and here we go life! Go get 'em!

There was no mission plan and most of us have no awareness of a desire to come into this world but here we are. We cannot even go back. We are left with no instructions on what we are supposed to do with this life. Things seem to just fall into place. We go to school, develop friendships. We develop as individual characters along the way but without a mission statement of what are we supposed to do with this life that has been entrusted to us.

As a kid growing up, I spent a lot of time walking over to my cousin's house to play basketball. It was during those long walks that I spent time pondering these questions. I felt as though God had a purpose for my existence but I really did not know what it was. At times I felt as though I was born encoded with a mission for my life but I could not recall what it was once I was born. It is almost as if I had been given a second chance at life on Earth but this time I was on a mission from God and I was going to have to go through this journey as Dimitry Frederique to figure it all out in the end.

So I spent my childhood seeking to find meaning to my life and I was living with a sense of an unfulfilled purpose. A lot of things that I did growing up were focused on finding that calling. I had repetitive visions in my dreams up until I was a teenager that I was destined for something great. I really did not want to miss it. I only saw these visions of success in my dreams. Nevertheless I never had parents who sat down with me and said, "we are going to teach you these values, we are going to install purpose into your life." I just dreamt of it.

And the visions were consistent just about every other night until my belief system bought into them that they were real and I could be someone of great importance one day.

In my teens, I had stopped dreaming but the visions were already part of me. It really did not matter that I could not dream any more in my sleep because those visions of who I would be one day were a part of who I was becoming in real life. They were imbedded as part of my purpose, my mission in life. I began to value my life because I knew that I was being called by God to do something greater than me. I started understanding certain philosophies about association that would later be reinforced in me through network marketing. I started valuing the safety of this precious life of mine. I learned to have respect for myself and the people around me.

That is when I began taking my life seriously. I made sure that I did not find myself hanging with the wrong crowd in school. I made a point of being attentive of my surroundings. This way I would not miss anything of importance to my future. I gained wisdom from those who were wiser than me. I became a good listener.

Along the way I had this burning desire to be a business man, to think outside the box. I was okay being the odd man out, who went against the status quo. I found my identity in high school. I was taught by a Jesuit priest who made me accept the fact that I was different and that I had a unique gift to offer the world. What I discovered was that I was surrounded by people who saw my potential and talent way before I fully understood what those talents were. I was destined for greatness and I believed it to be true.

At some point in my life I started to believe in myself. I started telling myself that I was a twice blessed man because growing up as a Catholic I was told that we all had a guardian angel protecting us. I knew that I was already blessed. My mother also told me that I was named by nuns in Haiti. These nuns are still in my mother's life even today. My mother was a teacher at a school for nuns back in Port-au-Prince, Haiti. Not only was I blessed once but I had women of God praying over my life at birth.

I later found out the origin and history of my first name. It was not by chance that I was called Dimity because even my name had significance and was unique. It is spelled with a Y not an I, like most people spell it. I found out that my name is commonly associated with the Greeks or Russian culture. Many times I have to tell people that I have a French background. The name Demetrius is very much associated with great scientist and astronomers. I myself would go on to college and study astronomy and later on philosophy.

Are you starting to get the importance of everything that you do to and for your child has significance? His or her name is part of the journey they will take. You cannot just take the life that you are creating lightly and give your child any stupid name without researching its meaning.

As an adult looking back, now I understand that I have always been an outlier. This is why I believed that I am destined for greatness. I do not say that out of arrogance but out of a belief system that was greater than me. I was also fortunate enough to have people in my life that were a blessing in disguise; my life did not always sound that great.

Back when I was a kid in Haiti, my mother and I got into a serious bus accident that left me handicapped. I could not walk straight. Doctors had told my mother that I would probably be in leg support braces for the rest of my life. But God had other plans, though, and my legs were healed. If you took a look at my IQ and potential for being somebody great, you would have passed me by in Haiti. I was very naïve and ignorant to the world when I was a kid. People could have easily called me a dummy and I would have accepted that as fact due to my circumstances. I was a straight D and F student because the education that I was getting was not working for me. Society would not have believed there was something great stirring inside of me. It was not until I came to America that I became a straight A and B student throughout grammar school, high school, and in college. The people in my country back then did not know what A.D.HD meant. Most have never heard of it. My environment was failing me but not my will to succeed. I was a timid kid, too, who was shy and soft spoken. Even today that is somewhat true but God saw my potential despite all of this and called me out at birth. My faith grew even stronger because I was a child of God's design.

You see, my purpose was already laid out. My only dilemma was that I had to believe that it would come true despite of all the struggles, frustrations, disappointments, and heart breaks that I would experience in the first thirty plus years of life.

I had an appointment with God at some point in my life and hope that I would become this great person in the world. I could easily have let the enemy defeat me during the course of my journey, aborting the vision that God had for my life.

I am a child of God and I have a purpose. God told me that I had a purpose. My mother, my god parents, my family, the church, my pastor, and my teachers - they all told me that I would be a man of significance one day. So why should I not, a Haitian descent, believe that I could make it in this world?

The only difference between you and I and the generation of children being raised up today is that I had a village of people who believed and instilled principles of purpose in my life since birth. Not everyone had those opportunities. This is the reason why most of us cannot be free to pursue our purpose, our dreams. It starts from the root of life. How can we pursue these dreams if we are never around as parents, guardians, mentors, or pastors to educate and inspire our children so that they too can become someone of significance? It cannot be done by one parent or one person in that child's life twenty-four-seven. It really does take a village to raise a child. Unfortunately, the world has us believing otherwise.

If you are someone who already has children, what is your purpose for living, breathing, existing? Better yet do you have a purpose for your child? Have you thought about the life that you want to give to your child? Have you spoken life into your children? If not, why haven't you started?

Do you think your child will find his or her purpose or calling on their own? The Bible says, "Train a child in the way he should go, and when he is old he will not return from it." (*Proverbs 22:6*)

Are you just having children because you want to or do you have a plan for that child's life? Do you have any plans to breathe your life's purpose into this child of yours or are you simply interested in being just a good parent? The sad truth about our society today is that raising a good child is not sufficient to ensure they have a life worth living.

One thing that you must understand is that your child needs guidance as soon as he or she is born. You must begin preparing your child to find his or her purpose by instilling certain principles into their life. There are a lot of personal development movies, animated cartoons, and books that you can find to teach them about seeking their purpose in life. But it is truly hard to do these things if you yourself have never understood the significance of knowing your own purpose in life.

The second thing you must understand is that most of us have never heard of personal development or have read one of these books unless someone had introduced you to network marketing, you yourself had indirectly picked one up by accident at the book store, or someone gave one to you. Today all I read is personal development books since I was introduced to them in 2001.

The irony of personal development is that you can easily pick them out once your mind has been open to something different. In my first successful MLM business, we were taught how to identify personal development examples in movies, music, or even a church sermon.

A great example is watching the movie Antz,[ii] Finding Nemo,[iii] or The Lion King[iv] with your child. All three of these movies are great examples towards helping your child understand the meaning of finding their purpose in life. There are thousands of other examples like these. All of them are focused on teaching your children personal development through a child's point of view via cartoons, musicals, kids' books, and short stories.

The next time you see them struggling to get the hang of something or you are trying to instill some of life's principles into them and they don't seem to get it, reference these three movies, Antz, Finding Nemo, and The Lion King. Let them know that even animals such as ants, fishes, and lions have a purpose.

The main characters in all three movies spent the first half of the movie seeking their purpose for living. It is the reason why they must start learning about finding their own purpose. It is never too late or they are never too young for you to start preparing them for their purpose.

We, as adults, are the ones who set limits in our kids because someone else did it to us at one point in time when we were kids ourselves. The cycle does not have to start in your family's legacy. You can be the one to change that in your child.

So here is the dilemma for those who have already given birth to a new life and was never thought about their purpose or that baby's purpose.

How can you understand what I am talking about if you have already aborted your purpose in life? How can you pass on the mission to your children if you do not have a connection with your Lord Jesus Christ?

In today's society, I see mothers who are lost, mothers who barely have a vision for themselves let alone their children, and they hardly know God - the Father Almighty.

2Corinthians 4:4 says, "The god of this age has blinded the minds of unbelievers, so that they cannot see the light of the gospel of the glory of Christ, who is the image of God."

Do you know what the "God of this age" is in this scripture? It's your jobs. Today a lot of us have walked away from the church and God's teachings. And we have passed on that acceptance to our children. That is why they, unbelievers, have a new master, their jobs. It's no longer God. Look around you today. Do you see what I am talking about? We have made our jobs our livelihood. Today a job is an extension of our children's freedom when they turn eighteen. I will explain later.

I want to stop right here and take this time to make a particular statement before we continue on.

Although this is a book about being an entrepreneur for the 21st century, I cannot help but talk about God for a minute. As you continue to read, you will see why this first chapter is important. I know some of you may find it offensive and uncomfortable, or better yet, not the politically correct thing to do anymore when it comes to writing a book. Please understand this point clearly. I am a man of God; I cannot help but give honor to my redeemer. I am not going to be politically correct (PC) throughout this book and I will not apologize for it as well.

Here is what you need to understand. I am starting the first chapter on the subject of "purpose" on purpose. There is a reason for that. I have watched this country run away from God. Yet we are all seeking to find significance on this Earth and trying so hard to do it without knowing your purpose.

Before you think of going to venture off on your own and start a business, you must realize that Joseph was successful because God was in favor of his success *(Genesis 39: 2-6)*. Some of us are successful in what we are doing but not happy because it was not the divine plan of God's doing. *Jeremiah 29: 11-14* says, "For I know the plans I have for you, "declares the LORD, "plans to prosper and not to harm you, plans to give you hope and a future. Then you will call upon me and come and pray to me, and I will listen to you. You will seek me and find me when you seek me with all your heart. I will be found by you," declares the LORD," and will bring you back from captivity. I will gather you from all the nations and places where I have banished you," declares the LORD, "and will bring you back to the place from which I carried you into exile."

Not until you are ready to establish this covenant with God will your purpose be found. It is not the other way around like most of us want to believe: "Once I have my life together, once plan A and B happens, when things settle down, I will start going to church, and then I will find favor in the Lord."

A lot of people today are lost like Thomas was in the Bible. Even our children in this era of babies raising babies are lost too, because we as parents have failed them; they do not know the way to salvation and their purpose in life because that mission was aborted from birth.

"Jesus answered, "I am the way and the truth and the life. No one comes to the Father except through me. If you really knew me, you would know my Father as well. From now on, you do know him and have seen him." *(John 14: 6 – 7)*

As the up and coming economic financial crisis gets worst within the next six years, more and more strangers will find themselves on their knees praying to God for the first time. It will not be any surprise as more and more people are searching to find jobs - as they are becoming scarce and far between.

So far I have heard people waiting up to two years or more to find a job since 2010. And I am talking about engineers with several degrees under their belts. I am not even talking about college graduates or folks without even a diploma.

Churches will be full to the max capacity in attendance, shelters, and other social services will be extremely busy, know that people will be scared and looking for hope.

And here you are again coming to the conclusion that "I" need to be in business for myself without first knowing something about your creator. It is truly an oxymoron.

Folks, you cannot run for freedom and have a desire to be free from your job without knowing who gave you spiritual life to begin with. You may have had a mother and a father who birth you into existence but you need to know your creator, the one who breathes life into your existence today. You need to know and have a relationship with the one who desires you to be free because not everyone was called by God to be free. Everyone heard the call in the womb but only a few accepted it and were chosen at birth. That's why this book is really not for everyone because everyone cannot become an entrepreneur and that's ok.

I remember when I was young and heard this phrase said often. "Every child that is born is God's attempt to create a perfect human being." Therefore, it is not by luck or by chance that you have this drive to be an entrepreneur. It was setup by divine purpose, beyond our comprehension. God has already seen your beginning and your end.

What you think is important now will not necessarily be important to you in your future. God does not care what your wants and desires are today but rather the paths that you need to take, that will lead you to your future purpose.

On October 11, 2009, my church invited a guest preacher by the name of Rev. Elias Ndeda from South Africa. He spoke about why some of us are not reaching a certain amount of success in our business. He went on to say that the reason why we did not get that million dollar deal was because we have unknown demons inside of us that will not come out until we have that success.

Let us stop escaping the source that is the light that guides us, the heat that keeps us warm. Let us seek rather the light that opens doors for us.

When it comes to knowing your purpose in life, the one thing that you don't want is living your life like the movie, *Gattaca*, where your life has been already predesigned by science and not God.

Gattaca is Andrew M. Niccol's vision in 1997 of a world that has no passion or creativity in pushing our youth towards reaching their full potential. *Gattaca* is a world that only allows genetics to dictate what our potential field of work will be.

How would you feel if DNA was the only thing that determined your place in this world? It's a world where there is no more imagination, no discoveries, and no appreciation of evolution by Mother Nature.

Logic is what defines our lives. How ironic is it that it was passion that innovated man to explore this world, use our imagination to create civilization, sculptures, art, and cathedrals all across the world, and put a man on the moon. Yet today, we are slowly allowing our jobs to become this fictional world called *Gattaca*. Why have you allowed your life to pass you by at a corner office or in a cubicle, suppressing your passion, your talents, and your hobbies that can potentially lead to a successful business?

In the end when it is all said and done, what kind of impact would you have made on this earth before you die? Would it be a life of regrets or one of accomplishments?

You're Life Cycle

A few years ago, I was at a business convention and Robert Kiyosaki was the featured speaker. He jokingly shared with us his definition of the cycle of life, which went like this:

> One day boy meets girl. Boy dates girl. Boy falls in love with girl and marries her. Now they start buying the liabilities. They get a nice car, a house, etc. He goes on to get a better paying job and is now making more money. The car is now upgraded, next comes the baby. He speaks to his financial adviser and he recommends that they buy a bigger house for the tax write offs. Suddenly the husband finds himself working extra hard to provide for his family. Along the road of life, he sees his financial adviser doing the same thing, stuck in the same rat race as he is. He is never home cause he is working long hours. Eventually he dies due to a heart attack and she is left with all the money. Well until she meets the gigolo and gets remarried.

Well, that is really the depiction of most of us in our lives - running the rat race to succeed by climbing that corporate ladder. The thinking is, if we work hard enough, we can get that raise or promotion. However, that does not always come true as we are passed for that promotion we always wanted or that raise.

There is, however, the other half of the population, living paycheck to paycheck each week, hoping for something better to come along. That was actually where my wife was mentally a few years ago; that got me to start writing this book.

My wife was asking herself if that was it for her life? Go to work, come home, and do it again every day of the week for fifty two weeks to be exact. Next, have kids, settle down, get married, and look forward to retirement. That was when the light bulb popped out as I tried to explain to her that it does not have to be like that. Most important, as a newlywed and an entrepreneur, there was no way I was going to allow this to be our future. I had worked too hard up to that point to just settle for a good job. I had seen the other side of success. I spent years rubbing shoulders with successful men and women; some were even in my age group, already having success. I knew that there was a better way than spending forty years working hard for somebody else just to collect a retirement check at the end. My only problem was making her believe that it is possible; that we can be successful people too.

Shortly after the fight with my wife, I had a very interesting conversation with my mother-in-law. I believe she asked me if I was happy. As I stood outside the front steps of the house, I paused for a moment to think about the future and I knew that I was not going to be content with my future if I followed in my mother-in-law's footsteps.

My in-laws were both retired. Living life at home and not really doing much, just enjoying retirement. In that moment of silence, I asked myself that question is that how I wanted to live my life in retirement? Better yet, I asked myself is that all my life was meant to be, getting married, having a family of my own, and one day retiring and looking forward to just playing with the grandkids.

For that moment in time I felt as though the world had stopped and I asked myself the very question that my wife had asked me: was that it for my life? Was that all we were meant for, to live our remaining years in solitude, travel, see grand kids, baby seat, and one day die? I had a bigger vision for my life and I did not want to accept her reality for one major reason. I knew that life was my parents and in-laws generation. It would never become my life for just one factor, retirement.

As an entrepreneur I knew that I would never get to enjoy the kind of retirement that my in-laws were enjoying, however small or comfortable it was. It could never be me because I knew what was going to happen to the baby boomers in a few years. My mother is still working a job and cannot afford to retire. I understood that I may never get a chance to enjoy retirement, working a job today. Those years that my parents and in-laws worked with a full retirement package are long gone. I knew that I could not expect to see a pension check, a social security, or even a 401K retirement check based on what I saw happening to our economy in 2008.

Even if I followed into that forty-forty-forty plan and retire, I knew I would still have to get another job just to supplement my income in my old age. Things were about to get a lot worse and I knew that the America we all have come to love and know so well was long gone.

The Pursuit of Happiness was Ordained by God
We are the only species with free will

"We hold these truths to be self-evident, that all men are created equal, that they are endowed by their Creator with certain unalienable Rights, that among these are Life, Liberty and the pursuit of Happiness. That to secure these rights, Governments are instituted among Men, deriving their just powers from the consent of the governed, That whenever any Form of Government becomes destructive of these ends, it is the Right of the People to alter or to abolish it, and to institute new Government, laying its foundation on such principles and organizing its powers in such form, as to them shall seem most likely to affect their Safety and Happiness....."

The United States' Declaration of Independence written primarily by Thomas Jefferson and adopted on July 4, 1776, by the Continental Congress.

Each year since its inception, we have proudly celebrated our independence from British rule. But what about our independence from ourselves – the United States of America? How far have we really come from those days up to now? It would take almost two hundred years from that signing of this declaration before slaves could be free yet they mention such words such as "all men are created equal," "life, liberty, and the pursuit of happiness." These words sound great but how realistic is the truth, how relevant to modern society?

As far as I can see, we have come a long way from pursuing happiness. Has not modern civilization captured us back into the slavery that is our office desk confined for eight hours a day or more? How happy can we be when half the world's population is hardly doing the things that their hearts had set them out to accomplish? Nonetheless we've allowed our emotional IQ to talk us out of pursuing those goals? Isn't that more self-evident than the real truth today? We have confine ourselves to an 8x8 jail cell we call a cubicle but we believe that we are free in spite of it all. Have we been removed from our happiness or the pursuit of our freedom for so long that we cannot tell when it has been taken away from us?

Wasn't it God that gave us our right to be free when His son, Jesus Christ, died for our sins? So how many more lives must be lost before we begin to acknowledge His will for our lives? Or have we become blind to realize that our children are becoming the next sacrificial lamb for society's need to repair its own broken system?

When I think about all of the other species on this planet, I can only say that ours is the only one with the free will to take our freedom back at any point in time. The big question is whether or not we want to fight for it or have we become so complacent that we have lost our way?

Maybe some of us have forgotten the words of our forefathers. It has been well over 230 years since anyone has been asked to dust off that old Declaration of Independence and read what this country fought for at one point in time. The illustration on the next page is from an email attachment that was sent to me many years ago; one that really depicts the difference of opinion on how we define the word FREEDOM.

Prison Vs. Work Rating

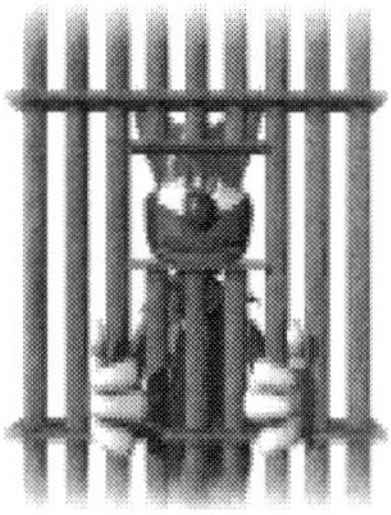

IN PRISON

you spend the majority of your time in an 8X10 cell.

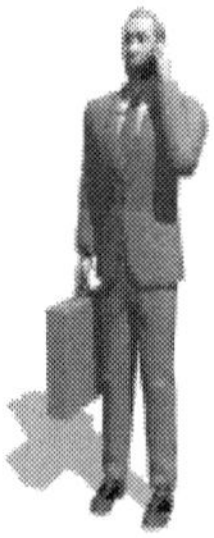

AT WORK

you spend most of your time in a 6X8 cubicle.

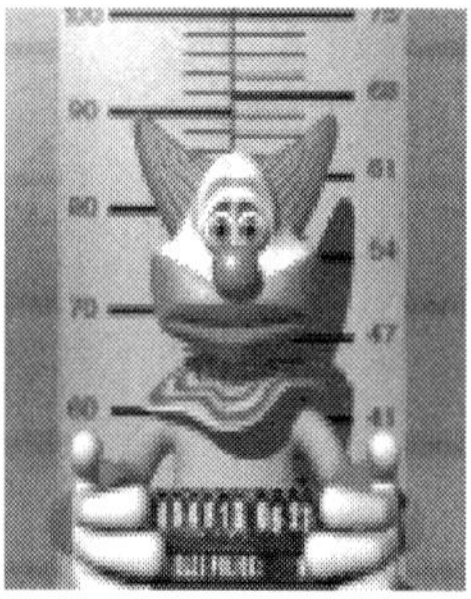

IN PRISON

you get three meals a day (free).

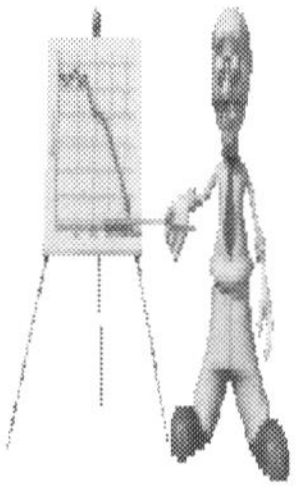

AT WORK

you only get a break for one meal and you have to pay for it yourself.

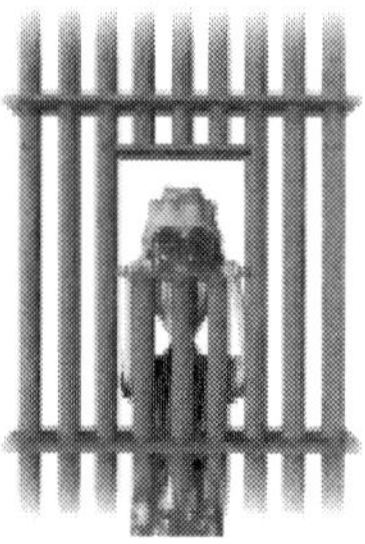

IN PRISON

you get time off for good behavior.

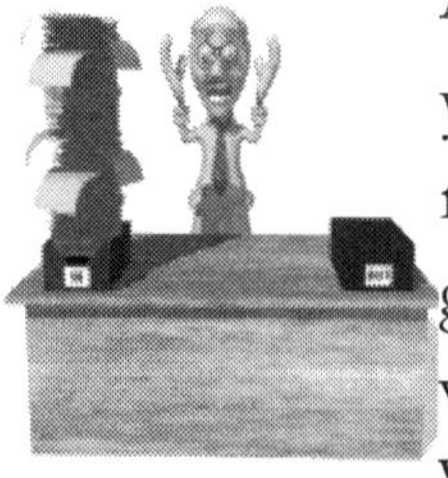

AT WORK

you get rewarded for good behavior with more WORK.

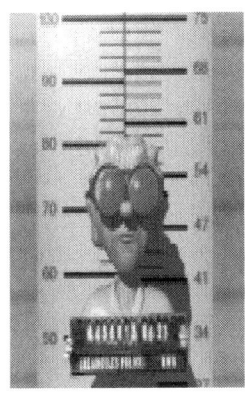

IN PRISON

a guard locks and unlocks the doors for you.

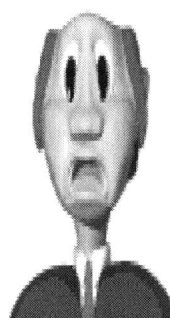

AT WORK

you must carry around a security card and unlock and open all the doors yourself.

IN PRISON

you can watch TV and play games.

AT WORK

you get fired for watching TV and playing games.

IN PRISON

you get your own toilet.

AT WORK

you have to share.

IN PRISON

they allow your family and friends to visit.

AT WORK

you cannot even speak to your family and friends.

IN PRISON

you spend most of your life looking through the bars from the inside wanting to get out.

AT WORK

you spend most of your time wanting to get out and go inside bars.

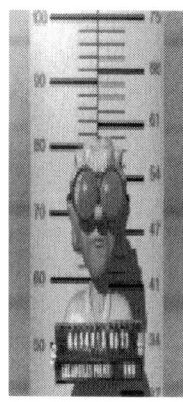

IN PRISON

all expenses are paid by taxpayers with no work at all.

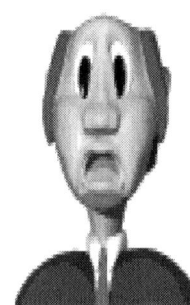

AT WORK

you get to pay all the expenses to go to work and then they deduct taxes from your salary to pay for the prisoners.

Humm?

Which Sounds Better?

Sometimes it is hard to know the difference if you do not look back in history and see how we got our start. If you are not careful, you might find yourself in a line up looking back at yourself.

The Pursuit of Happyness – the movie was written by Steve Conrad in 2006 as a powerful biography of the life and times of Chris Gardner, a family man who simply wanted a better life for his son. Here was a man who understood his full potential and was looking for an opportunity that could change his life forever. It did not matter that his wife aborted the mission, as long as his son was right there through it all with him. Chris Gardner was fighting for more than his life's purpose; he was fighting for his son's future.

Gardner was showing his son how to live a *Purpose Driven Life* by his example, conforming to his circumstances. Chris Gardner humbled himself so he could have what God had promised him from birth. What are you going to give up for your freedom today? You cannot claim your children's future as your personal sacrifice because the system already owns them. It's too late for them. They will never listen to you as an adult while you are a captive slave to your job too. The only option left is to start freeing your mind from bondage before you can help anyone else.

Even Srully Blotnick, who wrote a book in 1982 called *Getting Rich Your Own Way*, found after a twenty year study, that 83 out of the 1,057 participants who went on to become millionaires, all had a few things in common.

The overall consensus from his research determined that "great wealth can come to you only as a result of doing things you don't want to do." Meaning, that one thing you have been putting off because you think that it will not amount to any success might just be the thing that actually work in your favor.

Each one of the 83 participants eventually realized the very thing they determined was only a hobby was in fact their true calling / passion that God gave them. This was their key to ultimate wealth. It was not their careers or pursuit of worldly investments. It was simply their God given talents.

WHY DO BAD THINGS HAPPEN TO GOOD PEOPLE?

"God sometimes molds our character by allowing us to experience difficult circumstances." By Crown Ministries[vi]

There is a point in our lives where we find ourselves asking God, "why did you allow this to happen to me?" Either that, or we find ourselves blaming God for something we are growing through. And that is exactly what it is, a growth process. When it comes to God, the only time we "go" through stuff is when we do not learn anything from the situation in the first place. That is when we find ourselves repeating the same mistakes over and over again.

Based on my years of struggling to find my purpose in life, I have come to the conclusion that God always has a master plan for His children. We may not understand it at first but when the gloomy clouds have moved on, we do find understanding and meaning by looking back at the past.

For those of you who are going through some tough times right now, I want you to ask yourself this question: Have you ever come to the conclusion that in the midst of it all, that what you are going through right now is God seeking your attention?

Have you never considered that God wants to use your life's "his-story" as a testament of his good work?

Right now there are millions of good people in the world who have done everything right in their life but life itself just seems to have turned against them no matter what they thought was right or good in the world. No matter how hard they have worked, how healthy they might have tried to be; how much time they have put in this project, this job, this vision of their perfect life. Everything seems to be falling apart.

And why doesn't God pick on someone else? Someone who does not deserve a good life? Sometimes God will mold us to experience some temporary hardship, some difficult circumstances in life for His glory. Some of you have been so distracted by your mess, your pain, and suffering that you can sometimes miss what is right in front of your very eyes. God has been trying to birth out of you a new life, a new purpose, a new mission statement.

I want to share with you a couple of great stories of triumph that some of you may have read about along your journey. They are intended as a motivating factor to inspire you. Perhaps you have also witnessed the success of some of these people in the media, too.

Jesus of Nazareth — was preaching the word of God but we crucified him. He did not die in vain. I am still alive today because He sacrificed His life for me. He left behind twelve disciples who would change religion forever.

Alfred Nobel — invented the dynamite that cost the lives of many throughout history. He later made it his life's work to reward accomplishments that benefit humanity after a miss print in a newspaper describing his obituary instead of his brother's death. The obituary depicted the horrors of dynamite usage. He would go on to establish the Nobel Peace Prize.

Dr. Martin Luther King, Jr. — a preacher who changed the civil rights movement. He gave his life so that we would not have to be judged by the color of our skin. His dream still lives on in me long after he died. I am carrying his torch to the promise land and will pass it on to the next generation and so on. It is now up to us to finish the race ourselves.

Mary Kay Ash – She was a successful executive who reached the ranks of corporate America but was never accorded the same respect as her male counterparts. The glass ceiling motivated her to quit her job and started her own cosmetics company called Mary Kay Cosmetics. She went on to start a movement that would change the way women saw themselves, empowering them through entrepreneurship.

Harland C. Stonecipher – An insurance salesman in 1969 got into a head-on car accident that almost caused him to go bankrupt after being suit for an accident that was not his fault. His unforeseen legal troubles inspired him to create a little company out of Ada, OK, by the name of Prepaid Legal Services[vii] in 1972. This man's ordeal would change the way we view the legal system. He would go on to create a top notch multi-million dollar company and free thousands from their dead end jobs. As of August 2010, he has created well over 140 millionaires in his company to date. His tragedy indirectly changed my life as I was introduced to personal development because of his company.

Wilburn Smith – a local grocery store clerk in Ada, OK spent his whole life working there with the promise that he could purchase that grocery store when the owner retired. The owner never lived up to his promise. His disappointment led him to work for Mr. Stonecipher selling legal plans door to door. In the 1980s, someone came up with this crazy idea to change the company to a network marketing concept. Mr. Smith was asked to help lead the sales force. He went on to become a multi-millionaire with Prepaid legal Services and he himself went on to create several millionaires years later.

Dimitry Frederique – It feels like my whole life has been a never ending struggle, a constant battle to try and be the man I knew God had called me to be. A few years after John C. Maxwell wrote, *Failing Forward* in 2000, I began to understand how important my failures were for God's plans when I heard someone giving testimony about her own life experiences at a MLM convention. I would have never understood why my failures were so important to my future, if Maxwell never wrote his book. I would not have been able to write this chapter and convey to you why bad things happen to good people for a reason had I never taken the time to understand my own failures. So his book had an impact in my life indirectly. My mother was probably one of the women that was inspired by Mary Kay's cosmetics. She had the entrepreneur spirit within her while I was in the womb. So Mary Kay indirectly affected my life through my mother. I wrote the poem, "Who AM I" long before those words were a popular catch phrase in American pop culture because I had a revelation about my identity from attending the Million Man March on October 16, 1995. I remembered staying up pass midnight writing this poem in the New Africa House at UMass Amherst. I never forgot that day when it was complete. So Louis Farrakhan has an impact in my life. I knew this book was destined by God when I started writing it because I knew how many lives I would change because God knew my purpose. He knew that I was the one who needed to write it from my perspective, my struggles. When I came up with the title for this book, I could not find one search engine that had a book titled, why you must be an entrepreneur or specifically ask the question, Why Entrepreneurship? Once again I knew this was my calling.

On a side note: *even though one of my step daughters told me that she did not believe in God just before she moved out of the house at 19 years of age I knew in the end that it was God's will for her to believe that at her impressionable age because they are doing their own thing right now. Nevertheless I also know my Lord Jesus Christ will one day shine the light in her eyes and wake her up, before God let's all hell break loose in her life. For I know that God has a plan and a purpose for every one of us and the only way that she can learn from her mistakes is by growing through some stuff. I am comfortable today with her decision to move out because at 19 she does not know the God that I know; she does not know how God works his magic. In due season, she too will come to know the Lord like I do. So parents don't fret. At some point, they all will be running back to your arms when this economy changes and God says enough is enough. In due time your children will find their way back to faith if ever they lose it in their youth!*

On January 12, 2010 – Haiti was faced with a devastating earthquake. Many people that I have talked to after the event said that maybe the earthquake was a sort of blessing in disguise. Inevitably it will bring worldwide attention to Haiti, which was badly needed. This earthquake actually helped to rebuild Haiti, bringing change at last to the Haitian people.

No matter which way you look at it, in the end, the disaster has allowed Haiti to become a better and stronger country. Haiti's ordeal has definitely shown God what the world can do if we come together for a common purpose, a common cause. For the first time in history, so many countries came together in a live televised telethon across the world with more than 20 different networkers to ask for Haitian relief through donations on January 22, 2010. This act of kindness was indeed a testament of God's will to teach us compassion for one another.

MSNBC "Nightly News" with Brian Williams has a segment called

"Making a Difference[viii]" and they interviewed a man by the name of David Heim, from Ashland, Massachusetts, who experience firsthand the cost of drunk driving. An accident that left him paralyzed from the waist down and forced him to spend the rest of his life in a wheelchair. You would think that is where the story ends but that was 14 years ago.

Today David has used his misfortune to turn not only his life around but the lives of many others besides his.

On January 1998, David Heim founded The Wheelchair Recycler, Inc. in Marlborough, Massachusetts. A small nonprofit organization that is making news all across America for the work that his company does customizing wheelchairs for the less fortunate who cannot afford to buy a new one or afford the repair cost. Wheelchair Recycler simply uses old and used parts from other donated wheelchairs to repair and replace damaged ones.

David Heim also realized his purpose and goal in life was to make wheelchairs more mobile for individuals with various life style choices such as going to the beach, children being able to play on the grass, riding on dirt roads, riding in the snow, experiencing the outdoors etc. Today hundreds of people are living life to the fullest on a wheelchair thanks to the sacrifice David Heim made in 1995.

Now imagine if God spoke to you and told you that, for you to be successful and fulfill your life's destiny, you would have to live through a car crash and be paralyzed from the waist down. Not too many of us would sign up for that success story. Likewise God does not let any one of us go through stuff without knowing the outcome ahead of time. That's the magic of *Failing Forward*. Your struggles have meaning but it loses purpose when you don't reflect on your pain and suffering and try to make sense of why it happened to you.

I see a lot of people today brushing off their problems in life without any reflection on how they could improve things to avoid making the same mistakes over and over.

For those who find themselves in that boat often, you must realize that God will not allow you to move forward without addressing some issues in your life that must be resolved to have His glory. I have heard it said many times in various ways. You cannot achieve His glory with many demons walking behind you. You cannot be the same person with the same mindset hoping to resolve your financial issues, your relationship issues, or even your entrepreneurial desire.

You need to grow intellectually to find solutions to your current situation. You cannot keep facing the same problems dead on without searching for a new perspective on life.

That is why I love sayings like "two heads are better than one" and "if one door closes, another one is waiting to be open" but you have to continue to want to open the hundred other doors that are closed.

There is only one key to your financial success. You are the only variable to that key because it lies in your soul.

It is that burning desire to achieve more and become more. You cannot let a few doors hit you in the face and stop you dead on your journey. You have to start listening to your spirit to answer the question, "why?"

Why do I desire to be an entrepreneur, why am I never content with a paycheck, a job?

Why do "I" want to leave a legacy behind for my family?

What is the meaning for my life, for living?

What is my contribution to the world?

Those are questions only you can answer if you listen to your soul and begin to reflect on the talents God gave you. Then will you find the answers you seek.

I have spent a good portion of my life running away from my God given talents because I did not think they were good enough to make me successful. I have relied on traditional methods or other business ventures to fulfill my purpose. Nonetheless, I find myself back at the drawing board each and every time because it is not what God is calling for me to be.

Just like you, I saw my talent but never knew how to go about using it or making it come to flourishing. Others like myself were given multiple talents but choose to master only one, while neglecting the others. Meanwhile, God also gave us exceptional abilities, qualities that make us like no other human being. The majority of us allowed the authority of our parents to influence us and prevent us from fulfilling our dreams. Some of us have lived years in regrets while others rebelled and followed their passion.

For years, NBC's Jay Leno had a segment on his show called Stupid Human Tricks that I found amazing at times. For those who have never watched the show, Jay Leno would find average people for this segment who could do amazing things with their bodies, pets, and objects.

When I look at the people on that show, I am speechless at what gifts God left each one of us with to either amuse ourselves or find a way to make a living. And that is what's so unique about the show; people finding their gifts, talents, and sharing it with the rest of the world.

What you may have thought of as just a stupid thing that you can do, others have used it to create national recognition for themselves by mastering or honing in on a God given gift or talent.

If nothing else, they can say they were so good at what God gave them to do that they managed to get on the Jay Leno Show. That alone is an incredible story.

Nevertheless, to say incredible would be to do an injustice and undersell to what people can achieve on Ripley's Believe It or Not.

Some of the stories that I have read and seen on TV are amazing. And we could all be on that show if we used all of our God given talents. All that we were meant to be is hidden within us. Our potential is hidden in our childhood dream.

If there is any meaning or understanding in what I am trying to make you embrace about utilizing your talents and abilities, it is perhaps best conveyed by the science fiction show on NBC called HEROES![ix]

From the very first time it aired, folks who watched it got hooked on the show. At least I certainly was. They were a bunch of average people all across America with super human powers. All of them were scared and afraid of others finding out about what they can do with their hands or with their minds. The show is about how these individuals cope with what some would view as a monstrosity while others learn to live with their abilities to make a difference in the world. Nonetheless, each person is faced with a character flaw that holds them back from either using their powers or wishing that they were never given that ability in the first place. Of course, they are always the ones who are envious of those who have some God given gift – they are envious because they don't know how to take advantage of theirs.

Doesn't that sound familiar, though? We all have one or two hidden away. Your talent does not have to be stupid human tricks, as in the case of Jay Leno's show. They don't even have to be bizarre cases like you'll find on *Ripley's Believe It or Not*. They can be as simple as my talent for writing poetry. Although it is weird to see my persona and figure out that I love writing love poems, again, these are hidden talents for people like you and I. We have been pushing them to the side or never pursuing them as a profession. Being scared that we may not be good enough in the eyes of the world is just another FEAR, which is really false evidence appearing real. The reality of it all is, who cares? You can never please everybody. You have to always remember that everything is not for everybody; everybody is not for everything. Therefore, your talent can be as simple as being able to recite dates, events, and complex mathematical equations from just using your brain. It can even be as hard as being the first to discover a cure for AIDs or Cancer. As a matter of fact, it does not even have to be complex. Some of us love to create things with our hands, our minds, and our words. In essence to find your purpose does not require much from you but to think and reflect at what you have been good at all your life. In the end, you will find out that "IT" has been staring at you all this time in the mirror.

The science channel has a show on Sunday mornings called, *Built from Disaster*. The show is about how engineers use the knowledge learned from major engineering disasters of the past to design safer structures today. It answers the question very well. The only way for us to learn and move forward with innovation is to continue to improve our way of life. As the show title states, we learn from our mistakes. That is the best way to learn. The lessons stick out in our minds in ways that prevent us from ever forgetting them. Everything in America that has been man-made has been improved upon, due to our understanding of where we failed to see a future problem.

The following examples are the end results of the lessons learned from our past tragedies. Basic things like the white or yellow painted lines on every street were not invented until after Dr. June Hill Robertson McCarroll forced the laws to change in 1924 after having been run off the road by a truck in the middle of the night. Air bags in cars were not deemed necessary until enough data proved otherwise. There are countless examples to pick from to the more complex problems, such as the NASA Challenger accident, train derailments, airplane crashes, 2004 presidential election ballot failures with the infamous hanging chads, to Minnesota's bridge collapse in

2007.

A lot of people ask the question, why do bad things happen to good people when they themselves are faced with their own tragedy? It has been said that God will not answer your question in times of uncertainty because you are in the middle of your test. No answers will be given out to you until you have completed your test. God is seeking to instill something powerful in you. It is only after you have grown through your journey and had time to reflect, that you can seek out, through reflection, the answers and the reasons why God has allowed you to go through such an ordeal. God always keeps His purpose for you in mind. You may not understand it right now, at this point in time, but he knows, with time and wisdom his plan will be revealed to you.

On February 19th, 2010, I had the pleasure of attending a book signing for *G.r.o.w.* by Omékongo Dibinga. As he shared his journey to become a motivational speaker and poet, he later explained to me what forced him to take that leap of faith and start his own business. His testimony is really the reason why sometimes bad things must happen to good people for God to give birth to your full potential.

What I am talking about is how life will force you to move out of your comfort zone and to do something new, something better than what you may have limited yourself towards. In most cases, regardless if we wanted to or not, your life's purpose will find a way to move you towards your destiny. You just have to be willing to want it bad enough to go after it. Hence this is why Omékongo's story is worth mentioning here.

Up to 2005, Omékongo had worked as a school teacher out in the Maryland area. Like most people, he knew his potential as a teacher but was not being paid what he was worth. Furthermore, he knew that his boss, the director, would never allow one of their employees to be making more money than he did; no more than he would allow an employee to outshine him. So he eventually found out that his employer paid him ten thousand dollars less than what he was supposed to be paid. That event in itself forced Omékongo to evaluate his sense of worthiness and made the decision to leave and follow his dreams.

I was impressed by his story because that is actually the story of our lives every day. I know personally I have been through it in the past and you may be going through it right now yourself. But I have to ask you this question. What if he was indeed paid the ten thousand dollars? So what then? Was that all he was worth? The problem that was stirring inside would have never woken him up if the incident never took place. He would have missed his season for greatness just to be content with a bigger salary but an empty soul seeking to be free. So be thankful for some of the things you are growing through because it will force you to wake up and see a better future than the one you thought was good enough or as far as the ceiling goes. Always remember that God's kingdom neither has a glass ceiling, a limitation, or a time constraint for you to reach your full potential in life.

A good way to think about it is to look at people who are mysophobic or, as it is more commonly put, germ phobic. They are constantly washing their hands. But do you know that at some point in time, they can expose their body to more germs then they had intended. Why? Because they just over do it.

What they spend so much time trying to prevent eventually comes back to hurt them. We all know or should know that there are good germs and bad ones out there. But our bodies needs to be exposed to some of it some of the time, so that our body can be immune to it when we are older all of the time.

A friend telling you to wash your hands, especially in the era that we live in today, with issues such as swine flu and influenza, they are not wrong in what they are saying. The people who go overboard and begin to wash excessively are the ones you should watch out for. Likewise, a doctor who injects you with a vaccine or tells you that some germs are good for you is also right.

Case in point, have you ever considered what goes into a vaccine to protect you from such things as snake bites, influenza, and swine flu? It is the very thing that can kill you. I am not a doctor but I understand that the very thing that can harm you can also cure you. Initial test trials are usually done on animals to expose them to illnesses, so that they are able to create a cure that will heal the very thing that is causing pain.

Your immune system has all that it needs to fight for you. Unfortunately, we do not always have to pay the price to get to the correct formula and begin trail runs on humans. We use mice as our initial test subjects before we try it on ourselves.

Isn't it a miracle, though, that we find it hard to believe that God has already created us with all the things that we need, including abilities, and the potential to go and follow our dreams?

On a side note: *sometimes we find ourselves so dependent on drugs and other substances to take away the pain rather than using what nature has to offer. After a while, our bodies become immune to the basic things in the earth that can save us.*

If anything, our creator has already put all the people in your life that you are going to need to make success happen for you. That is why we use the word, network. The reason you have never thought of it is because you have never worn your business hat and begin changing your mindset to see it for what it is, networking.

How ironic is it that direct selling (a practice that most of us despise) is basically what networkers refer to as network marketing. But it is the very thing all of us have been doing all of our lives.

By the time we reach eighteen, we have spoken to or known over 1,000 people. If you do not believe me, look at your cell phone, Facebook, MySpace, LinkedIn, and Twitter pages. They are all networks that you created for fun but they can also be used for business. I will get to that towards the end of the book.

In the Mist of It All

With regard to our jobs, I clearly understand that we all need one to survive, especially if you do not come from money and have had to work for what you have today. But some of us need to know what it is like to work in an awful job environment so we can be disgusted by the notion of someone else handing us a paycheck and telling us that is all that we are worth. Too many of us are simply too comfortable where we are in life, our jobs, and our titles that we never change on the inside out.

For some of us, the system is designed so that we can appreciate the process but most importantly so that we can push ourselves forward and say, "that will never be me again, that will never be the situation my family has to be in to survive. I am worth more than what my job it is paying me. I can achieve greater things by using my potential, my gifting, and use my skills to start my own business."

At some point in your life, and I hope it is not towards the end, you will be so disgusted with your current situation, you will be forced to change it. Your spirit will not take it anymore and you will be left with no choice but to venture out into the world of unknown possibilities called entrepreneurship.

That was where I was in 2000-2001. I remember the mornings that I did not want to even get up out of bed to go to work but I did because I felt obligated.

I was growing through some things in my life at the time that I did not know would be the motivation that I would need later on to push myself out of my depression. The very thing that I had loved to do, IT, I was no longer passionate about it. I was beginning to want more out of my life than just a job. I did not want to be in a dead end job and wondering about my God-given gifts, my potential, and my desires to be self-employed.

I use to get to the parking lot at my job and sit in the car trying to motivate myself to get into the office.

When I lived in Springfield Massachusetts, I use to listen to a radio station that was being broadcast from Hartford, Connecticut on my way to work. I would arrive in my office parking lot at the same time every day, at the point in the radio broadcast when they would repeat this saying. To most folks who listened each day, it was nothing. To me it was an uplifting feeling, a word of encouragement, and a great motivator to go into work and fake it for eight hours. That was what I did each day until I moved back to Boston in 2001.

Today I cannot even recall what that saying was but it was part of their morning show routine that helped me get through that tough period in my life.

A month or two later, I would get into another network marketing company that changed my life forever. That personal situation that I had gone through became my strong why, as well. It led me to generate rapid success in a tough market place. It was also the first time that I found a true network marketing company that I could embrace and learn so much from. It was that same company in which I found mentors, increased my understanding of business, and increased my financial IQ. Still, it took me *Failing Forward* and not giving up to get to that stage in my life. Today I am more proud of my failures in life than I am of the success to come because I truly understand the relevance of my failures. They are my stepping stones to success. I no longer see my failures as bad things that happen to good people like me.

Keys to Your Success

I have come to realize that my life struggles were the keys to my success. You and I, we all have them. The irony is that the same keys to our success are also the same keys from our failures. The difference between you and I is in the way we use those keys; whether we open the right doors with them or close the wrong ones in our life. Most people throughout the world see failure as something they should shy away from or simply forget about. But we alone cannot be blamed for it. Look at how our education system is setup. If we fail, we get an F. There are no second chances although life gives us plenty of opportunities for them. God gives us plenty of second chances, too. Where would we be if we did not have them in our lives? Many discoveries were found as the end result of those second chances - mistakes that would have never been discovered were it not for failure and failure being somewhat acceptable. So why is it that all we do is try to avoid looking deeper at the mistakes we have made in our daily lives for us to progress and grow intellectually?

The answer is quite obvious. We have never been taught by our parents, our teachers, and even ourselves that *Failing Forward* is really the key to our success. We are not really taught that failures are not really setbacks but lessons about your life that can help you later on. But do you really respect your failures enough to see them as wisdoms that can help you succeed later on? Or are you someone that never reflected about why you are growing through a certain situation? Is your whole life a big "why me" excuse or are you taking the time to learn from each mistake you've made?

I personally have never allowed myself to repeat the same mistakes twice and for one simple reason: I take the time to learn from my errors in life so that I don't ever have to repeat them.

Do you ever find yourself repeating the same mistakes over and over again? Do you ever take the time to ask yourself why is that? The answer is really because you do not reflect on them. You never planned to review. You simply kept moving on in life without giving your mistakes any thoughts. That's why you find yourself repeating them over and over again until you start to pay attention to them and ask yourself why is your life stuck like a broken record that cannot pass this hurdle in life? Nine out of ten times, it is because we failed to review our pass mistakes and take out the valuable lessons learned from them.

IT'S BIBLICAL

Did you know that God left us with a lot of great examples in the Bible of those who thought they hadn't amount to anything in life when he called them out?

A few years ago, someone forward me an anonymous email entitled, "God's People Failed along the Way Too." The author of this email wanted everyone to know that God had selected others just like us who have failed in life or along the journey. Some of the folks below did not even think they were worthy to be called by God. Nevertheless, God individually picked each one of these folks, despite of their weaknesses and made them great. So do you really have an excuse when you look at where you have been today? Better yet, is your story within these Biblical[x] stories? Can you identify with someone on this list?

By Faith
(Hebrews 11: 1-40)

ABRAHAM was 99 years old when God called upon him to lead …. but by faith, he kept his covenant with God and became the father of many nations. Genesis 17: 1-27; Hebrews 11: 8-10

SARAH was barren in her old age…. but by faith, she was able to bear a son, Isaac. Genesis 21: 2-7; Hebrews 11: 11

JOSEPH was abused and betrayed by his brothers because of his visions.... but by faith, he fulfilled his prophesy, was made second in command over all of Egypt, and saved his entire family during a time of famine. Genesis 37: 2-36; Genesis 3: 1-23; Genesis 41: 1-57

MOSES was a stutter and did not believe that he had the leadership skills needed to help free God's people.... but by faith, he freed the Israelites and parted the Red Sea. Exodus 12: 31-42; Exodus 13: 17-22; Exodus 14: 15-28

GIDEON was outnumbered on the battlefield, fighting against the Midianites.... but by faith, Gideon was able to defeat 32,000 men with only 300 men. Judges 7: 1-23

RAHAB was a prostitute.... but by faith, her life was spared Joshua 2: 1-21, Joshua 6:17

SAMSON had a weakness for women.... but by faith, he prayed to God for strength and destroyed the temple of the Philistines. Judges 16

JEREMIAH thought he was too young and shy to do God's will... but by faith, he became a prophet over all the nations. Jeremiah 1: 6-10

DAVID had an affair and was a murderer.... but by faith, he became king and a man after God's own heart. 2 Samuel 11: 2-6; 2 Samuel 11: 14-17; 1Samuel 13: 13-14

NOAH was a righteous man who was cursed and ridiculed for

building an ark.... but by faith, the ark saved his family and a new covenant with God was established. Genesis 6: 9-22; Hebrews 11:7

JONAH ran from God and was swallowed by a huge fish.... but by faith, God delivered him to Nineveh to fulfill his purpose. Jonah 1: 1-3, 17; Jonah 2; Jonah 3: 1-3

JOB lost all he had and became bankrupt but did not curse God.... but by faith, he believed God and was blessed more in the latter part of his life than the first. Book of Job

PETER denied Christ.... but by faith, he became the leader of the Apostle. Mark 14: 18-31; Mark 14: 66-72; Acts 2: 17-21

The DISCIPLES fell asleep while praying.... but by faith, they went on to spread the gospel. Luke 22: 39-46

JESUS recruited 12 ordinary men.... but by faith, they received the Holy Spirit and spread the gospel across the world and launched the largest religious network ever. Acts 1

ZACCHEUS was the scoundrel tax collector.... but by faith, he had lunch with Jesus and was saved. Luke 18: 10-14; Luke 19: 1-10

TIMOTHY was a young man who experienced stomach problems.... but by faith, he was called to be a disciple and preached alongside of Apostle Paul. 1 Timothy 5:23

LAZARUS was dead.... But by faith, God had favor on his soul to raise him from the dead. Luke 16: 19–31

JESUS the Son of God…. but by faith, we call him Abba Father. God manifested in there persons, God the Father, God the Son and God the Holy Spirit. Genesis 1; Romans 8: 15

And it is by faith that God knows that you will make it if you try. Therefore what else can be said, all the excuses have been taken out. All you have to do now is trust in him that he will provide you with all that you need to succeed in the future. The part of you that is lacking in skills, we'll let God worry about that. The Lord will find someone to help you along the way. You just have to get started. You can read what God did with "The Widow's Oil" in (*2 Kings 4: 1-7*) to understand that once you hear your calling from your Lord Jesus Christ, the rest will take care of itself in due time.

Did you know that God had already preordained 2,350 verses in the Bible to deal with money and finances? He had already planned this just so you can get back into the word. And what's amazing about the whole thing is that the scripture passages are still relevant even today. So God's words are timeless. So you really have nothing to fear about your lack of knowledge about business. The answers and guidance are right in the bible. There are Christian base people and companies around that can help you fill the gaps. Go online and search for them. God never left you empty handed. He has been waiting patiently for you to come back to him. He has been waiting for you to come to terms with his purpose in your life so that you can help him finish building his kingdom. That is all God has been asking of you from birth.

Now that you are starting to believe in yourself, I must warn you that it is not going to be easy. There is going to be a sacrifice and a commitment from you that is necessary in order for you to be successful. "For God so loved the world that he gave his one and only Son, that whoever believed in him shall not perish but have eternal life" (*John 3:16*). God gave his life for us so we can have life and have it more abundantly. So it is our right to pursue happiness in the gifting that was entrusted to us. Not what society said you should become or your parents think is necessarily best for you because it is the right career that nets you in the highest income bracket. Instead of pursuing our own dreams, we have allowed man to enslave us again by way of debt and increasingly higher taxes year after year. When are we going to be the wiser one to say I will not allow this form of slavery to continue on in my family? Will it take another generation to set your family free or will you wake up and realize that God has already paid the ultimate price for your freedom?

By seeking and fulfilling our purpose we are starting to do God's work. Fulfilling His purpose means that you are serving God's will for your life and not man's will on to you. And that is exactly what (*Colossians 3: 23-24*) is saying. So when we avoid or shut down our true calling in life, we are closing the door to God. You are really saying, "I am going to reach success on my own. God does not really need to play a role in my life."

"For we are God's workmanship, created in Christ Jesus to do good works, which God prepared in advance for us to do." (*Ephesians 2:10*) Why would God put that specifically in the Bible? There was a reason and purpose for it. God had already planned what he needed you to do with your life. It is by faith that you will accomplish all things through him. So why have you been ignoring your talent? It is not by chance that you can do what you do. You were chosen by design. The reason why you are unhappy with your career and jumping from job to job is that you are not following your heart's desire. You are thinking that your crazy idea or talent is not good enough or that you cannot support yourself on that income because you have a lifestyle to maintain.

Ask yourself which is of greater value to you – your happiness or the security blanket of what you are doing right now to pay the bills? I can guarantee you that if you pursue what you love with all your passion, the love you have alone will carry you beyond your wildest dreams of financial success. This is where this book comes in to help you put on your entrepreneur hat and start thinking like an entrepreneur. You will begin to see things that you have never considered before. Your eyes will be open up to a world of opportunities that you could not have imagined was possible through entrepreneurship. And if your hesitation is because you are scared to take the leap of faith, well this book has many valid points about the future that will scare you enough to start now. There are plenty of other reasons why you must live beyond your existence and change your legacy at the same time.

IT TAKES ONLY ONE OF YOU

When I was a kid growing up in America, I use to ask myself whether or not I really believed that I was chosen by God to do something great with my life. Like most kids at my age, I saw the world being so big that I doubted whether or not I could be of such an impact to the world. That all changed one day when I picked up a pamphlet and read what it said. I cannot recall if it came from one of the Jehovah Witnesses passing out pamphlets or someone from the Church of Jesus Christ of Latter - Day Saints that gave it to me. Regardless of who gave it to me, the message has stayed with me my whole life.

It goes something like this. In order for me to make a difference in the world, I should start with the planet. Well the planet is too big, so I should start with my country. Since the country is too big, I will start with my state. Since my state is too big, I will start with city. Since my city is too big, I will start with my neighborhood. Since my neighborhood is too big, I will start with myself first at home.

Many times we feel like the task that God has called us out to do is too big for us to handle. That we are only one person with limited resources to accomplish anything worthy of the world's attention. And I am here to tell you otherwise. Below is a list of individuals who have changed the world as one person but with a lot of support behind the scenes. They are no different than you and I. Each one had gone through their own struggles along the way but they made it.

Michael J. Jackson, Arthur R. Ashe, Jr., Eldrick T. "Tiger" Woods, Thomas C. Lasorda, Henry L. "Hank" Aaron, Jack R. "Jackie" Robinson, Michael J.

Jordan, Michael G."Mike" Tyson, James "Buster" Douglas, Neil A. Armstrong, Marilyn Monroe, James J. Brown, Jr., Elvis A. Presley, "Madonna" L. Ciccone, Jesse L. Jackson, Sr., Rosa Louise McCauley Parks, Anthony Jerome "Spud" Webb, Earvin "Magic" Johnson Jr., Dr. Martin Luther King Jr., Malcolm Little "X," Harriet Tubman, Frederick Douglas, Louis Farrakhan, Jesus "Christ" of Nazareth, Mahatma K. Gandhi, Mother Teresa, Muhammad Ali, William Jefferson "Bill" Clinton, Abraham Lincoln, John F. "Jack" Kennedy, Nelson R. Mandela, Barack H. Obama II, William H. "Bill" Gates III, Michael S. Dell, Steven P. Jobs, Lawrence J. "Larry" Ellison, William Nelson Joy, Stephen G."Woz" Wozniak, Sergey M. Brin, Lawrence "Larry" Page, Mark E. Zuckerberg, Albert Einstein, Harland C. Stonecipher, Darnel Self, Delxino Wilson de Briano, Oprah G. Winfrey, Jim Rohn, Donald J. Trump, Robert T. Kiyosaki, Hilary Hinton "Zig" Ziglar, John D. Rockefeller, Steven A. Spielberg, Shelton J. "Spike" Lee, Annelies M. "Anne" Frank, Thomas J. "Tom" Brokaw, Daniel I. "Dan" Rather, Jr., Wolfgang Amadeus Mozart, Warren E. Buffett, Larry J. Bird, William F. "Bill" Russell, Andrew Carnegie, Henry Ford, Samuel M. "Sam" Walton, Shawn Corey Carter aka "Jay Z", Sean John Combs aka "P. Diddy,"Russell W. Simmons, Walter E. "Walt" Disney, Mary K. Ash, John E. Walsh, Sir Richard C. Nicholas Branson, Jay V. Andel, and Richard DeVos, Sr.,etc.

This list could easily have gone on and on. These are just a few of the people who have changed the world. You name the industry, there are always one or two names that stand out. It really takes only one person to make a difference. You do not have to be famous to make a difference in the world. God is the only one keeping count. There are more unsung heroes making a difference than there are celebrities doing the work.

On November 8th 2009, Pastor Matthew Thompson gave a sermon at Jubilee Christian Church on the story of Gideon, who was called by God to fight the Midianites. Gideon, who gathered 32,000 men, was ready to go to war but the Lord stopped him and said, "You have too many men for me to deliver Midian into their hands" (*Judges 7: 1-10*). In the end, Gideon was left with only 300 men but God told him that was all that he needed to achieve his glory.

It's a good lesson for us today because we all have baggage, too many baggage called stuff; too many bad experiences and failures that are really holding us back from reaching our purpose.

We make excuses for why we cannot accomplish things. My mother and father has never been successful, my grandparents have never made it this far financially. Why should I believe that I can go further than they have? Everyone has doubts. Do you question your abilities because you are, perhaps, a high school dropout or a college dropout, because you only got so far with something before?

Only God know your full potential. Never let man determine the limits of God's vision for you or society as a hole. They did not create you with a purpose and a vision, God did.

Like the Midianites, God does not care how many issues you have going on in your life. It is despite of all these things in your life that you will be magnified in His glory when he calls upon you.

Who Am I

Who am I
When I was just an egg in my mother's womb?
Who am I
When I was born into slavery?
Am I just 3/4 of a person?
Who am I
Seconds before I was born?
Who am I
Before I was named?

Who am I,
I am Dimitry Frederique.
I am unique
Who am I,
I am an intellectual man.
Who am I,
I am an educator.
Who am I,
I am the greatest.
Who am I,
I am the forgotten.
Who am I,
I am the unknown.
Who am I,
I am the pride & tears of joy from my mother's eyes.

Who am I,
I am spiritual.
Who am I,
I am a leader.
Who am I,
I am a human being.
Who am I,
I am great & beautiful

Who am I,
I am the oppressed.
Who am I,
I am the hope.
Who am I,
I am the future.
Who am I,
I am a child of God.
Who am I,
I am the dream of Dr. Martin Luther King's, " I have a dream "

Who am I,
I am destined for greatness.
Who am I,
I am the chosen one.
Who am I,
I am the peace maker.
Who am I,
I am the abolitionist.
Who am I,
I am a scientist, an Astronomer, & a Computer Scientist.

Who am I,
I am the star that shines brightly in the sky.
Who am I,
I am compassionate.
Who am I,
I am talented.
Who am I,
I am God on the cross.
Who am I,
I am a Catholic.
Who am I,
I am the messenger from God.

Who am I,
I am the loneliness in your eyes.

Who am I,

I am the poor.
Who am I,
I am freedom.
Who am I,
I am an honorable man.
Who am I,
I am justice.
Who am I,
I am a dreamer.
Who am I,
I am a thinker of the 21st century
Who am I,
I am a renaissance man.
Who am I,
I am a knight in shining armor.
Who am I,
I am a man stuck between two worlds.
Who am I,
I am the heart-broken.
Who am I,
I am the shattered dreams of a drive-by shooting.

Who am I,
I am history.
Who am I,
I am the one million man of the Million Man March.
Who am I,
I am that dream of the Million Man March.
Who am I,
I am the big brother and big sister.
Who am I,
I am a poet.
Who am I,
I am a biracial child.
Who am I,
I am the past, present, & future.

Who Am I?
I am, therefore I am an educated man.

Who are you?

Last but not least,
I am a black man,
A descendent of Haitian & African slaves.
So before you look at my skin color,
Look at my credentials & love me for who I am!

I wrote this poem in 1996 after attending the Million Man March because I understood how important it was to establish my identity. I had spent many years reflecting on who I was as a person, as a human being that it was not hard to address the struggles that we all go through to make it in this world. This poem today is so fitting with a generation of kids growing up, hardly knowing who they are, what they stand for, or what they believe in any more.

In the process of finding yourself, I hope you take the time to define who you are, what is it that you stand for in life? This way no one can sway you from the journey you are about to take. You do not need to become or be like anybody else. God made you just how you are. You must hold on to your inner strength to know that you have something unique to give back to the world. It only takes one of you to start changing your his-story.

A CAREER-MINDED WOMAN

On any given work week, you can go to downtown Boston or any major city, for that matter, and find yourself a sophisticated, highly intelligent woman heading into work.

With her high heels on, a power suit, a touch of makeup to accentuate her beauty but not too flashy. She is the ideal corporate executive trying to move up that corporate ladder so she could prove to herself and others that she is indeed good enough to be considered as part of the crème de la crème in her field.

On occasion you can find her plaques somewhere in her office with all those accolades and degrees she has earned. She holds in her arsenal a master's degree, a business degree, top honors in her graduating class, and even some times, a PhD. But those things do not please her. All she is looking for is a little respect and recognition as a woman. All that she is asking for is a fair chance to be paid what her male counterparts are being paid.

As a young man, these were the types of women I saw often and thought were very successful. As an adult who has worked closely and observed these women, I see now a different side to their world.

I used to see successful women moving up in the world and I used to think they had truly been given a chance to shine. Not any more. Now I know it is not all that glamorous, holding those "respectable" positions.

What I see now is really a different type of "glass ceiling" - one that is raised a little higher than most but it's still there. It's perhaps more daunting, in fact, because it is the type of ceiling that leaves "respectable" women with no choice but to get those degrees and honors; she has to put in all that work just to have a chance of being considered, then she has to always out-work her colleges, just to have a chance at being respected.

Because she has been surrounded by testosterone for so long, she has forgotten what it means to be a lady. She has even been labeled a "bitch", simply for being a tough business women. To fit in, she had to put up with the derogatory statements, the cussing, and the degrading comments towards other women in her office. For the most part she could only smile or add to it so she could be labeled as one of the fellas. She cannot complain about her feet hurting in those high heel pumps. She cannot get emotional or whine as a woman could during her menstrual cycle. She can never have a bad hair day. She can never have a personal off day or display an emotional breakdown. She must look and act the part every day.

On any given week she is hard at work and is rarely seen taking a lunch break let alone a fifteen minute break of her own choosing. She is always the last one out and the first one in the office. She burns the candle on either end. She is always on her game; always on top of things. She may know more than her bosses but she makes sure she does not over step her boundaries and out shine them.

On occasion, she fines room to socialize and go out on a few dates. Nothing is ever serious until she finds the "right" one.

Although she does not mix her business with pleasure, you can hardly tell when she is in a relationship of any kind. A woman of her stature has an image to uphold.

Eventually she gets married and find herself with an earlier than planned pregnancy. To her, it is one setback that she can readjust her schedule for and work around it until the baby is born. In her mind she will work up to the last month before delivering.

The typical motherly bond that one would feel when giving birth for the first time is not usually felt by such a high profile executive of her stature. In most cases the reality sets in not during delivery but after she holds that baby in her arms for the first time. Prior to seeing her baby for the first time, her motherly instincts do not set in because she is usually too busy to notice that a life was in fact growing inside of her. It did not become real to her until she laid eyes on her that a bond is created. That's when everything stops. The ambitious goals to continue climbing that corporate ladder, working late, and living that fancy lifestyle all of a sudden don't seem that important any more.

For the first time she begins to realize and cherish the life that she holds in her arms is indeed a precious child of God. She is beginning to understand the meaning and purpose of her life. Her world as she knows it has changed. During her maternity leave she is beginning to understand how precious and fragile the life that she has just created is. She too is reevaluating the purpose of her own life, her own job. It is at this moment that she realized that she cannot go back to that same life that she was so accustom to. The busy work days and those long sixty to eighty hour work weeks cannot be her life any more. And it is usually towards the end of her maternity leave that she realizes and has concluded that she has not been following her heart and purpose for her life. She has been putting off her passion or that business idea for years until now.

It is at this point in time that she discovers her life's purpose and how she can create a home base business of her own so that she can spend more quality time with her baby. She is not ready to leave her child with a stranger. She knows that her baby needs her as much as possible.

Each and every time I hear these words, "she is not coming back" in the office or hear it said over the phone, I know what they are referring to. It puts a smile on my face because I know that the woman in question has found her calling. This top notch executive mother has given up the high life so she can be at home with her newborn. She has accepted her role as a new mother to instill certain life principles into her child. She has realized that she cannot be an absentee mother in her child's life in exchange for a corner office. The life of her baby is more important than any job. In the end, she has learned to put on her creative hat on and find a way to make a living from home while still making a difference in the real world. Once again, life has forced her to be her own independent boss without losing her self-respect and self-image as an intelligent woman. That in essence is a true career minded woman.

I stayed up late one night to watch a movie called *"Baby Boom"* which was released in 1987. It was directed by Charles Shyer and starred Diane Keaton as a successful corporate executive who was bypassed for a partnership at her firm. This movie is truly a great representation of what corporate women go through at their job. In the movie, Diane Keaton found her entrepreneurial spirit when she was stuck with a baby. She eventually left her demanding executive job and moved to Vermont. She created a simple product to support herself called "Country Baby" that led to her becoming a very successful business owner.

Once again, here is a movie showing the world what a mother can do if she takes all that effort from her 9-to-5 and put it into her creativity. The end result is always a successful mother giving birth to her life's purpose when she puts her mind to it. It is a movie that every hard working woman in a corporate environment should watch, just for the ending. The statement that the central character makes to her old boss is worth listening to as well. She left her old life behind, telling the corporate board, "you will have to find another person to run the rat race for you."

BABIES RAISING BABIES

It is only through our faith in God's vision for our future that we can begin to accomplish great things in His Holy name. Pastor Matthew Thompson[xi] gave a sermon on November 22, 2009, entitled, "Your Life, Your Race, by Faith." It was one of his best sermons ever, based on (*Hebrews 11: 1-40*). In his message, he asked the question: How can we pass on the baton to our children when they are living life without any purpose?

When I see this generation of children raising children at such a young age it alarms me for several reasons. For one they have lost something that is so precious to life's existence when they decide to pass on the responsibility of raising their own kids to their grandparents or mothers. They have robbed their childhood from gaining any wisdom by becoming a parent themselves. In the process of raising a new born, they have to manage work, their social life if any, trying to finish school, and often enough finding a new place to live.

When I was a teenager, I understood the value of life. It is my personal belief that no one can really appreciate the value of their life until they hold one of their own children in their arms. As an adult today, I may not have a child of my own yet but I understood that concept so clearly at an early age. It is why I could never take someone else's life. But for these young kids who grow up raised by children, at some point along life's journey, there is a loss of hope and respect for human life. Too many of these inner city kids have lost hope and respect for their own life because they are too busy raising each other. A life, eventually, is nothing worth cherishing since they themselves never had a chance to be a kid.

Life has been hard from the very beginning and they live a cycle of oppression that will haunt their family tree for generations to come. It is hard to escape an endless cycle that requires a teenager to raise another life that is now dependent on that mother or father to teach them the same values and morals they were once taught in life. Now how can these teenage parents do that if they never gave themselves time to grow up and become an adult themselves? Once one generation thinks it is ok to be having children when they themselves are immature children incapable of taking care of themselves that in itself is a child who has the odds against him.

It was only a few years ago, I remembered, that a youth pastor working in the prison ministry at his church, shared this information with me about the mentality of today's youth. He said that young men who are currently incarcerated are defining their manhood by shooting someone or serving time in jail. All I could think, when I heard this, was how sad it was to have this little "value" for life and fail at God's purpose.

In the minds of some of these kids, surrounded by violence, it is easier to take the life of someone else than to consider their own purpose in life. That's why there were so many drive-by shootings in the 1980s and 1990s. That's why there was so much black on black crime. That's why you have the highest death rates amongst teenagers today who cannot even live long enough to see their parents get old. That's why you have the Columbine shootings and the rise of high school shootings all across America's high schools today. No one cared enough back then because it was declared a black or minority problem.

At the turn of the century, it no longer became a minority problem. It is not something that can be over looked, but an American problem that must be addressed. What was once a phenomenon in the black culture has spread out to all races, ethnicities, and religious belief systems. There is no one teenager who is immune to the violence or the babies raising babies syndrome. It is part of their day to day culture. They live it, breath it, and see it in the school grounds. What's worse, they chat about it, text it, YouTube it, MySpace it, or Facebook it as if it was the drama of the week.

Most of these kids have never known what love is. They are not being taught that their life is important. No one is really teaching them to have goals and to strive for more out of life; to make something of themselves. How can they really learn when we, as parents, are in our own struggle and suffering? How can they learn these things when parents are financially strapped and forced to work long hours and extra shifts just so they can provide for their families? How can they learn all these things when some of our parents today have lost hope themselves? How can they reach their full potential when we, the parents, have given up on our dreams in exchange for "a safe secure job with benefits?" Being enslaved to your job was never part of God's original design. God called us to be entrepreneurs.

The majority of these girls and boys today are seeking the agape kind of love that they are yearning for from their biological father or from God, by dating early so they can feel loved the way a father and mother should be teaching them. Instead, what they are getting are young immature boys under twenty years of age trying to show their love by having a young teenager spread her legs. Meanwhile the only time they know how to express the word "love" to these young girls is when they have ejaculated with an orgasm-leaving these young ladies feeling empty and rejected only to resent the new life that is now inside of them. So a new cycle has started. Now they are a single mom and alone never to have known the meaning of agape love from a father or the one God had planned for their life. That young girl begins to resent even her son. He in turns grows up never knowing the love of his father; never learning the fundamentals of being a man or a father one day. Today we see one generation after another being born without a father figure in the household. After a while it becomes the norm-the standard for which we have settled for. And the next generation after that will grow up never knowing his or her purpose in life because of that missing void. A child is born every couple of seconds without ever knowing his or her father but most importantly, never understanding their purpose in life because they have lost some basic fundamentals of life from the very beginning. This begs repeating again because "every child that is born is God's attempt to create a perfect human being." So when you have an absentee father or a lack of parenting in the home, you must realize why the ball is being dropped each and every time.

That's why I believe that entrepreneurship is the key to changing everything. As entrepreneurs, parents can inspire hope and good work ethics from the fruits of their labor. Wisdom, knowledge, and wealth principles can be passed on, from generation to generation, when the spirit of entrepreneurship is instilled in our children at an early age.

But it is truly hard for you to pass on those values when all you can do is think about making ends meet, living paycheck to paycheck, wondering if you would have a job tomorrow, or a roof over your head. It is hard, I understand that but you must also understand this point. The new generation of kids today have thrown away the Barbie dolls for a real life like doll of their own. Fully funded and subsidized by the government as financial hostage for future slave labor. Meanwhile these young baby producers are claiming their new born as their getaway ticket for public housing and a stimulus check. It's all tied up and gift wrapped in what they call their 18th birthday surprise. It's the new and improved teenage rite of passage they call freedom but in actuality it's an invisible seal to their coffins sixty-five years later. These kids have prostituted their babies for what they think is benefits when in fact they are government welfare checks to imprison their minds and souls. For the next thirty years they will remain enslaved. Once they have awakened and have seen the errors of their ways, they will spend another thirty years undoing the shackles that had bound them into a false sense of job security in the first place. However it is already too late for their offspring because eighteen years would have passed and they too will be prostituting babies of their own.

Eventually it will become an endless cycle with no end in sight. If we don't set about reviving the spirit of entrepreneurship in America, the implications of continuing on our current path are very grave. This issue is not a minority problem as one would like to think. Rather it is an American epidemic that is going to be worse off than the baby boomers spike in over population growth. Never mind the demise of the baby boomers in 2015, in fifty years it is going to be twice as bad for their grandchildren's generation if nothing is done about the out pouring of kids being born without proper child care and financial support to take care of them.

Furthermore the main reason behind this epidemic is because our jobs have enslaved both parents to a 9-to-5 work week. Since the 90s it has become harder for a two family household to have a stay at home wife. No one working a J.O.B has the time freedom to enjoy the life they have created. It is becoming harder and harder for parents to take the time to instill morals, a dose of common sense, and values in their children simply because their parents no longer have the time to do it. The system today has both parents out of the house chasing down a dollar bill. Meanwhile they are losing the war to win their children's souls and save them in time before they turn eighteen. Hence leaving the enemy to take over our children's lives only to force the ideals and principles of family values out the window. The system does it each week by enslaving you and then your eighteen year old child into thinking that they need a job so they can be free from the discipline of their parents.

Unfortunately, in our society today more and more women are

content raising their kids in a single family household without always considering the long term effect on a child without a father figure. But there are a lot of children being raised up feeling a void in their life.

As a man, how can I attempt at becoming an entrepreneur myself without ever taking the time to know where the desire came from? Was it from my mother or my father? For the majority of my life I did not have an answer to that question. The reason being is that I did not have a relationship with my father either. However it took me finally taking the time out of my life to do some soul searching, asking myself those unanswered questions - who is this man that gave birth to me? Who gave me this gift or talent? For some of us, we have abilities to do incredible things due to the gifting that was passed down to us from either our father or mother. However it is hard for us to horn in on it or bring it out of us because that parent is missing out of our lives. Other times, no one is able to see your child's potential because we are too busy working or distracted by life's demanding schedule to spend that quality time with them. What I discovered about my father was that the drive, my temperament, the unwillingness to quit, and fight for what I believe in came from his spirit. My kindness, my passion, my intellect, and my love for poetry came from my mother's spirit. Together they formed my character. And I could not be myself if I did not have either one of them within me or better yet understand how each one of those spirits work together. Sadly, there are children being born today that will never get those same opportunities that I got.

So I ask you what has been missing in your life up to now that has been preventing you from reaching your full potential? Is it closure from a loved one, is it that missing parent in your life, or have you not had a chance to listen to what your heart has been telling you to do with your life? God has been waiting on you to reach this point in time. Stop doubting yourself.

On a side note: *it took me thirty-three years to understand this important concept before I would find my wife. The very thing that was a part of me, I was fighting it my whole life because I did not understand it. Today I have come to embrace both of my talents and gifts so I can use them to reach my full potential. Just from that concept alone, I came to understand the meaning of the phrase, "you are what you marry!" In the end, I chose to marry my strengths and not my weaknesses.*

Can you comprehend the point being made here? It's like having a Bill Gates without the creator of DOS or Steve Ballmer to create Microsoft. It's like having a Steve Jobs without a Steve Wozniak to create Apple Computers or Sonny and Cher to form a duo singing group. One cannot be without the other in mention. That is how important both parents are to a child's life yet society has made it the ok thing when it comes to having children. So much so that we have a lost generation of babies raising babies without the vaguest idea of what it means to be a parent. We have made them think that it is easy. One parent is good enough, I can do it all by myself. That is the words I hear kids speaking today which they heard from their parents before them without even knowing the situation that led to their own decision. The ideals of parenthood has somehow been outsourced through government aides, community centers, a welfare check, government housing, free daycare, free diapers program, free clothes, free shelters, or drop-off points where you can leave your unwanted babies. All of these programs have been subsidized by our tax dollars at work. However all of these free services have come at a cost to the hard working Americans of today and the reenlistment of a new form of slavery that I call economic slavery at its best. I will explain in the next chapter.

The Missing Link

One day I happened to have stumbled upon this show on WeTV called, "The Locator." It is a show about bringing families together. Their focus is around grown adults who had lost contact with their biological parents at a young age. In fact, the sole purpose of the show is to find people's birth parents.

As I was watching the show, I noticed a trend occurring. All of these strangers with various lives were sharing the same story of feeling an emptiness in their lives, a missing piece, or feeling incomplete having been raised up without knowing their biological father or mother. Each story was unique in itself but they all solidified the point that I am trying to get across to you in this chapter. Knowing who our biological parents are or were in our childhood plays an important role in finding our purpose in life. Without that key element or perspective of the pass, we can be wondering for years as to why we are still struggling to find our place on this Earth.

One of my good friends found out that her father was not her biological father. In fact, it was not until she was in her mid-forties that she found out who her biological father was. The family kept it a secret for years. She found out that she was a product of rape. Her mother was raped by someone she knew.

As she went to college and pursued a career in business law and ventures into entrepreneurship, she found herself loving the pursuit of music and the entertainment world while combining it with her law degree. She spent a good portion of her adult life perfecting these skills but there was always that empty void that she could not answer. As she learned more about her biological father, she discovered where her talent for entertainment and music came from. He had a successful career in entertainment working with well-known actors and major film stars.

Although she could not fix the past, she does regret those lost years that she could not get back for not knowing about her real father or the missing link to her past. Nevertheless she has learned to appreciate a part of her that was incomplete and has filled that void as to who she is and where her interest and talents came from. Despite of the circumstances relating to her birth, her biological father died before she could meet him, but she thanks God for the opportunity to have closed an unknown chapter of her life.

WHERE ARE ALL THE LEADERS AT?

I know that *Matthew 20:26* says, "… whoever wants to become great among you must be your servant," but too many of us are just followers and not even servants that can rise amongst the many to become leaders. There are so few Godly people being raised up to do the honorable things these days. Part of our problem in society today is due to the level of corruption taking place in corporate America which has trickled down into our day to day interactions with one another. And the problems stems from the lack of leadership around.

As a parent, we should be the ones teaching our children to be the leaders of the future. But if we are not able to raise our children right, where else are we going to get these leaders from? The role models we use to look up to are all dead if not just a dying breed in the 21st century. Many of our 20th century icons of American culture are dying of old age or illnesses. Those role models have long been forgotten as classic shows like, *"Leave it to Beaver."*

At an early stage in life, we cannot tell whether or not a child is already gifted or talented. That is why we all should be instilling these principles in them at an early age. Don't wait until they have grown past ten years of age to say, well Johnny is gifted. It might just be too late. Some of us can tell base on our own abilities, our own genetic makeup. Those of you who are leaders already know what I am talking about. I believe that leadership is genetically encoded into our children because it is passed on from generation after generation. What tends to happen is that someone in the blood line ignored that gift or gets side tracked from their purpose. Furthermore this child's ability remains dormant or skips one generation completely.

In my years in business, I have learned to understand the saying, you are what you marry. And honestly, that was something I personally struggled to understand for many years. I was going after the wrong things and I did not realize it until I was in my late thirties. I am a born leader and I have always recognized that about myself but you could not tell sometimes, from the women I dated. Here I was looking for a wife in these women that I had dated and it never would work out. Most of my relationships did not last long because I always felt something was missing. I didn't realize what the problem was until two years before I found my wife. The majority of the women I dated lacked leadership qualities or skills that I have and truly valued. It was right in front of me my whole life and I never saw that until I took the time to really reflect on the problem. My wife, on the other hand, is a born leader. She cannot help taking charge of things just like I do. Nonetheless this is where the conflict laid within me for over thirty years. My mother never had leadership qualities but my father did. She may have had the entrepreneurial mind but did not have the backbone needed to take it to the next level. It's like the Steve Jobs and Steve Wozniak story of Apple Computer that I have already mentioned above. They needed each other to be successful.

Now here is where the dilemma of our society rest. Most of us, just like me, never know who our parents are or were. A growing percentage live an incomplete life because we did not get to know our parents. Most of us are failing to fulfill our purpose in life because we missed the role models who were supposed to teach us about ourselves. For some of us, it has been ignored not just one generation but hundreds of generations before your birth. Some of us have never found a mentor to pull us aside and say, you have potential. I see your gift. I see a great leader in you. Hence that is where network marketing comes in. That is why I am an advocate of becoming a professional network marketer in the 21st century. There is still hope but you will never find it at your job.

At my church service I have listened to both of my bishop's sons, Matthew and Andy Thompson, speak about how they too are now raising their kids to become leaders. Some of us reading this part right now do not understand how POWERFUL of a statement that is. They are both raising leaders for tomorrow.

I have been preparing my future son or daughter for their role on this Earth as leaders. I have been planning my children's birth all my life, too. I know my calling and my purpose is to make sure that they attain their rightful place by my side as leaders. That is and will always be one of my purposes as a father to my children. I speak of it before they ever existed. Why is that so important?

My wife and I breathe life into our future children just about every day. Let me be clear, by no means are we pregnant with child as I write this. But if you were around us on an ordinary day, you would find us making jokes about their characteristics because my wife and I know that we are born leaders. We may not be thinking about leadership literately but we already know what our children's behaviors will be. We know of our own habits when we were little kids and how our personalities began to display leadership roles as toddlers. That is powerful. We are setting the stage for a fruitful life. Ones that they will carry with them into adulthood and pass it on to their children one day.

I can only speak for myself when I say this but all my life I have always wanted to have a son. Not because I am a male and that is what we usually want. It's because I know and see that there are too few men out there that are willing to step up as father figures, as mentors, or become that great leader that our community needs today.

How many men can we say are great role models? How many are great leaders, family men, or a great role model for our children? There is not one that comes to mind. And no, rappers, sport stars, and reality TV personalities do not count! Al Sharpton, Jesse Jackson, and the likes do not count either. It is not because I do not believe them to be leaders. Our children today need roles models and leaders in their generation to step up. Mr. Sharpton and Mr. Jackson are both leaders from my parents' generation, the boomer generation. Therefore I need to prepare my son to be one of the few around for his age group. Our children need to see role models their age doing the right things, being pillars in their communities. Dressing the part; not wearing baggy pants hanging off their butt cheeks nor seeing young girls dressing so provocatively that you cannot tell if they are heading to school or coming out of the club scene at 7:00 AM. Nor wearing spandex; showing off their chest at a job interview, or the corporate office. They need to see saved families at home, at church, and in the public eye doing it proudly. They do not need false role models; men who inspire kids to become champion golfers one day but then go and cheat on their wives on national television the next day. They don't need to see a strong black role model being carried off to jail for rape or drug possession - that undermines the whole idea of the role model. They also do not need to see someone they have looked up to being handcuffed and dragged out of the office for embezzling money or on national television explaining their alleged tax evasion.

I know I am speaking from a black perspective right now but trust me my fellow Caucasian, Asian, Jewish, or any other culture that I may have missed. Your children are not exempt from that life style that our society portrays as normal. I see it every day. These issues that I am speaking of impact every corner of our global culture, ever ethnic and racial group. Your children are being influenced, too. Neither your money nor your success can entirely shelter them from the aroma of what feels good and looks cool. A matter of fact, it really makes it worse because you are not around. You are always too busy being at the office to even pay attention.

Our children need examples of leadership in all cultures. Being broke and struggling, living paycheck to paycheck is not a great example. That is why it is so easy for them to be captivated by the glamour of celebrities and sport stars. Who else are they going to model after when we as parents have failed them? Too stressed out worrying if you are going to have a job tomorrow is not the way to win them back. Never mind not knowing where your next meal is going to come from because you are at your wits end after having been laid off for the third time. You are always crying broke yet you still have a job does not set a great example either. Telling your kid that "we cannot afford it" has been ingrained in their head at such a young age that they began saying it too without any effort as adults. Saying to yourself right now as you read this chapter that teaching your kids to be leaders is the last thing on your mind when you are always living for today, is never going to solve the real problems facing your family. Believing that your own life is such a mess that you cannot even think about tomorrow will never set them free for the next generation that will come regardless if you want grand children or not. So in the end, who is left to pass the baton? Who is going to look after our children's future? Is it you the parent who is only living for today and tomorrow; never to look into the future and ask the provoking question, "there has got to be a better way to live than being in the mess that I am in right now?"

CHAPTER 2

The Price We Pay for
Freedom & Security

THE IDIOT BOX

Back before television became mainstream, children and even young adults seem to have been much more active and involved in different activities – various hobbies and outdoor play, for instance. As television became more diverse with literally hundreds of channels available, mindless TV watching seemed to have taken over. Back in the 1950s everyone had some form of responsibility or another. Even kids had chores and other activities that kept them busy after school. There was not a whole lot of programming back then to entertain them for hours like we have today. Therefore the invention of television was not that important to anyone at the time. By the time we hit the 1960s and 1970s, the invention of color television spread fast and new programming came a long that caught the attention of folks who found themselves being entertained at home in front of a box rather than going out to have fun. Children who use to playtime now found themselves watching things like Sesame Street, Leave it to Beaver, Lassie, and other family programs who were among the few television shows that showed some educational value back then.

In moderation, of course, television programming can be hugely educational, but the 24/7 idiot box access is not. We caught the news in real time and watched family oriented shows that focus on morals and values. We all knew what time it was when the station identification siren came on. By the 1980s and 1990s, the networks created programs that were broadcasting past midnight and soon enough we found ourselves watching that idiot box 24 hours a day.

Our great grandparents saw what the invention of television was going to do to our children and they were right. We got addicted to them. However they were ahead of their time when they coin television, "the idiot box." If only they could see what television has evolved into, is both shocking and shameful.

With the invention of the porn channels, movie channels, soap opera channels, sports channels, and reality television, it is no wonder we have become an overweight nation battling things like record incidences of heart diseases, diabetes, and adult and childhood obesity.

Even the news today is watered down. Much of it has very little to do with hard facts. Between January & February of 2010, I watched two late night comedians Jay Leno & Conan O'Brien battle it out for the prime time spot light at 11:35pm. A much younger generation now finds the news boring. So in order for our youth to stay somewhat informed, they have to be entertained at the same time. Today there are more late night shows popping up than ever before. Comedians like Jon Stewart, Stephen Colbert, Russell Brand, and Bill Maher have reinvented their careers by providing your children "pop culture" news. It usually consist of a quick 30 seconds of the real news attach with satire as the punch line. Saturday Night Live have even seen their ratings and popularity go through the roof simply by offering a comical view of former Presidents like George W. Bush, Jr. and other political news headlines. Sadly enough that has become our youth's definition of the news.

More seriously, though, when it comes to business news, the stock market, broadcasting networks like CNN, CNBC, or Bloomberg Television, there is nothing funny about the way economic data is being delivered to you. The numbers portrayed on television can be quite deceptive, depending on the source of the information. When you look at the economic data that came out prior to the housing bubble of 2008 or the jobs numbers post-2008, they are usually so detached from the reality we are living. If anything, these numbers tend to be a lagging indicator of what is really happening. But investors like yourself buy into these numbers as always factual when in fact they are misleading.

I remember watching CNBC reporters, for example, talking about how unemployment rates were improving. Television is so often used as a propaganda machine, disseminating soft news to ease your concerns and quiet your doubts. The same scenario played out prior to the stock market crashing. If I recall clearly, just about every commentator was telling investors to buy more. There was no full disclosure at the time. Only Marc Cuban stuck his neck out and avidly went against the norm and said that he was sitting on the sideline. He stated publically that he was staying out of the stock market. No one really listened. Remember, though, it may look good or sound good but you better do your homework before you drink the Kool-Aid. The average investor must understand that these numbers don't really mean much to you because you are really relying on people who come on the air with a nice suit and tie, with a smile on their face telling you what you want to hear. And that is really how the average person makes a buying decision. Now if you were an educated investor that does his or her research, you will not be easily fooled at the numbers. Always remember these words, "buy the rumor, sell the news." Big institutions have access to more information than can be converted into print for the masses to read it, see it on TV, or hear about it on the radio. Let's face it, full disclosure or insider trading is hardly enforced. By the time the consumer gets the news, it's already old. The market sentiments may have gone backwards or moved ahead. In the financial crisis that we are in right now, I am warning you to be very careful about what you buy into when you hear such optimistic news in the marketplace. There is a lot of "fuzzy math" going on with the job numbers.

There are a lot of hard working Americans today who do not have a clue as to what is happening with the unemployment numbers. And why would they, when they are told that jobless claims are down or 1 million jobs have been added to the economy? The question is where are they? And how come we cannot find at least one employer who wants to hire me?

Well the fact of the matter is, you need to understand what is happening behind the scene for those of you who have been without work for at least two or more years. To make the numbers look good, companies are only hiring some people on a part time basis or as contract workers. They can claim that people are working. And what about the millions of jobs being created? Well, there are one million new jobs being put out there. Unfortunately, most of these jobs are for workers that have particular skills – particularly new, technology related skills. Skills that you do not qualify for. The new jobs you hear about in the news are predominantly for a 21st century workforce that has the latest trainings, fresh out of college.

If you listen carefully to what is being said, you will start realizing how often they mention "new skills," going back to school," or "getting retrained" as parts of the strategy to get these new jobs. But what if you are over 50 years of age, close to retirement? As the saying goes, it's hard to teach an old dog new tricks. And the new tricks are all computer-base or automated by machines.

So who does these new jobs help? A new generation of employees, governmental statistics, and politicians who look good in their respective states. They also benefit corporations as well. It protects them from having to go out and hire full-time employees for two main reasons. The first reason is that they are protected from having to be obligated to employees who are hired full time since they would have rights and legal claims via the fair labor laws and practices under the company's union or HR department. The second reason is that they do not have to pay them any benefits which actually cost them too much to keep you. So it is a lot easier to rehire you on a part time basis than full time.

If the economy tanks again, it is easier to get rid of a part-time worker. They actually don't owe you, the employee, any explanation because you were hired on a part-time or temporary basis such as a contract to hire. Today most people do not realize that they were hired as an "employee at will" or have yet to understand the meaning behind those words. It is the legal term that gives employers the right to terminate your employment at any time, regardless of your tenure.

Another major factor that makes the unemployment numbers look good is that some folks are not really getting any more benefits. They do not qualify for benefits any more or they have maxed out on the government allotted unemployment benefits. All these factors take these unemployed folks out of the government's statistics. These folks are left empty handed with no more options but possibly welfare. The media have you believing that unemployment is really going down. Everybody gets optimistic again and wants you to buy into the lie that we are in an economic recovery when we are far from coming close to recovering from anything. Meanwhile everybody goes back to their fairytale lives believing that we are going to be okay. Jobs are coming back. The government will save them. The economy is getting better.

I am no expert on the market but I really think that some common sense is necessary when evaluating the U.S economy as a whole. Do your due diligence and research. Talk to the people, the neighbors, your friends who are still unemployed and ask them, how is it going for them? They will tell you otherwise. I will go further into this in "The Fake Out Period" chapter in part 3.

As I have previously stated, the media does not always cover the whole truth. It has a tendency of showing only fragmented segments squeezed into a two to five minutes of air time.

These days you may find yourself having to go online to even get snippets of the truth about a particular event or the full story as directed. Sadly, though, many of us will buy into the idiot box because we do not read as much as we use to. We do not do research or know how to research information properly, even with the internet at our disposal. We simply take everything we are told at face value.

One thing that we tend to forget is that the global media today is controlled by a small group of companies. Only a handful of newspapers and television networks are actually independent of these companies still. The majority of media outlets are owned and operated by the conglomerate of companies that control what is said or allowed to air on TV and the newspapers. So much for freedom of speech!

CONDITIONING THE STATE OF MIND

As a foreigner in this great land, I never took for granted the opportunity that God gave me to come to America. Being born a Haitian, I knew that *No Condition is Permanent*[xii]. I am very thankful that my family made the sacrifice to come here. I am grateful for my freedom and the chance to pay it forward one day.

As I got older, I began to understand, too, why foreigners like myself have called this land of opportunity. I can see it all around me yet others cannot see the same opportunities that I see because it has become clear to me that their state of mind has been conditioned to accept an alternative reality. Maybe I see it more clearly than others because I have come from nothing. I can see the difference between the shackles that held me down in a poor country like Haiti vs. the invisible shackles that American-born citizens have wrapped around their feet.

Although the United States was founded on the principals of freedom and democracy, the country has changed its collective mentality over time; most of the citizens today are dependent. The nation itself has a dependent mentality and is crippled by it.

Most of us have heard the phrase, "There is nothing that comes free in America." Why, then, do we have a sense of entitlement today? Maybe the problem goes back to that idiot box that I mentioned earlier.

After I got married I noticed that my wife would routinely come home and just watch TV. She was the typical couch potato. Unlike her, I had a business that I was building so I did not have time to hang out after work in front of the TV. I was out building my business. That was my routine.

We had two different philosophies on life and the difference came down to the idiot box that had been conditioning my wife over time to just be a couch potato.

In fact, she was being bombarded by commercials on TV. She was subliminally taking in these sales ads left and right, without even realizing it. Instead of being a producer in life, she was learning to become a consumer.

I discovered over a period of time that my wife was no different from any other household in America. Long were the days that you worked as an indentured servant-worked for free to learn a skill so that you can start your own business. There was no idle time for television or having our children be raised on TV. Everyone was busy. There was no coming home to lie around. But times have changed. In fact, we all have become commercialized to a sales speech on TV. For some of us, every day is a sales special at our favorite store. We get hyped to go and buy because we really believe that the company is offering a sale.

Every major outlet store has a coupon or discount that you can now get with a gift card or store card. It's no longer about paying cash. It's almost impolite now to offer cash as a gift. You have to put it in an expiring gift card. You can even gift one to a friend with a swipe of a credit card. Meanwhile you hardly pay attention to the interest rate charges and card fees you pay at the counter. We are indebted consumers of materialistic things that we really do not need. Yet we go to work complaining about our jobs all day and go home to do the same thing again the next day. Never to think about starting a home base business or creating our dream job.

My friend Rudolph and I have had many discussions about the complacency that we tend to find ourselves in at times, even as business owners. We all get into a routine from time to time and find ourselves stuck in lazy mode. We get home from work and turn on that television to find our favorite show instead of reading a book to grow our intelligence; instead of continuing to work on our plan B.

This is why it is so easy to go to work for someone else and punch in a clock eight hours a day. It takes commitment to do the thing we set out to do long after the mood we have said it in has left us. In other words, we have to rage a war against ourselves to stay focus on our goals. It is not easy to do it on your own without some form of motivation to keep you going. And that is why we say in Network Marketing to have a workout partner to push you. I will get back to that point in a later chapter.

What is security?

When we look back at the American Dream, we realize that there was in fact a price that we paid to have access to the freedom that we have today. You hardly hear people talk about the American Dream that much anymore but I am sure it is still a goal many still attempt to achieve. By the way, what is the American Dream today? Maybe the American Dream of our parents was just that, a dream about living in a big house with a picket fence and 2.5 kids. Still, it is just another false idealism that most Americans believed in. It is no different from that idealism of a safe secure job with benefits. It does not exist anymore but we are still working hard for it. What I see today as the real American Dream is buying into that status quo like we all are taught to do and stretch a dollar every day to live up to that fantasy.

We grow up seeking our independence. We buy with our eyes what our wallets and bank account cannot afford. The upgraded cars come next and soon enough the babies are right behind. Sometimes they are usually unexpected and they don't always follow in that perfect order. And we do all this with one job, trying to make ends meet. Now our purpose for living is no longer about enjoying life and the pursuit of happiness but rather living to pay for all the luxuries. We have become so dependent upon keeping a job just to pay for all of those liabilities. At times some of us will have a boss that is aware of this and start making your life a living hell just out of spite or envy. Some of us are no longer able to enjoy the luxuries of life because we are working twice as hard to keep it. A large majority will get a second job in an attempt to maintain that comfortable life style. The extra cars, the yacht, the boat, and the vacation home – these things are rarely used. We feel good for having them. If anything, it is our definition of achievement and no one else's. Some would argue, we are not trying to live up to the Jones. We are the Joneses. Life is always good until the money stops coming in. And that is where the problem lies; your income alone is what's providing for all of this life style and nothing else. It goes back to that famous saying; "don't put all your eggs in one basket." When we think of that saying, we only relate it to our stocks and retirement accounts, i.e. 401K. We never think about making that philosophy true for the jobs that we are committed to.

Speaking of the Joneses, there is an actual movie called the Joneses, created in 2009 and starring Demi Moore and David Duchovny. The two actors are hired contractors that pretends to be a family living the high life. Their sole purpose is to get others in the neighborhood to buy the products that they have. Paying top dollar to keep up with what is in reality a factious life. It is a very interesting movie that actually makes us look back at our American Dream philosophy. Is there an American Dream left to be admired or only a nation of debtors?

The elephant story that I want to share with you right now can shed some light on the topic. It is no different than the five ton elephant at the office. Have you ever seen an elephant at the zoo? It looks very happy doing tricks to entertain us doesn't it? But that elephant has been conditioned by its master into captivity. We may not see its shackles but they were there at one point. Changes to the elephant's the state of mind have also occurred. It has been conditioned to believe that this is it for its life. He no longer struggles or fights to be freed. Yet the chains are off. Since birth, these giant beasts were in captivity. Chained up to prevent from escaping. As they got older, they became accustomed to that chain. Never to resist or fight back. That baby elephant has grown up over time to accept his condition - the chain as a permanent fixture on its leg. It never makes an attempt to free itself as an adult. In time that elephant's spirit has been crushed. It has no desire to escape even though the chains have been removed. It does not know the difference any more. All it knows now is how to do tricks and be merry.

Doesn't that sound like our own lives on the job? I have another story that might be closer to home. At one point in time, I was hired as an IT consultant to come and fix a lady's virus-infected PC. She was a family woman whose husband had just come home from work. She had picked up the kids from school on her way home. They were a typical hard working family.

As I was working on their family computer she went on to start cooking dinner while the husband went about his business. The children were in front of the television trying to do homework at the same time. In between their chores, mom or dad was checking on their children's homework. That seemed to be their regular routine. One that they have mastered over the years. There was little time for socializing or communicating. And that was the problem with that scene. You barely have time for yourself. You are just heading to bed or starting to wine down by ten or eleven o'clock. And back up we are the next day to repeat the process.

While others can relate to family life, we all have held a job before and understand the environments we have been forced at some point in time to work in. In September 2009, I happened to be working at an Adolescent Center in a hospital's check in counter. It just so happened that I ended up spending four hours working on a computer problem there that day and was able to see what goes on in an Adolescent Center on a typical day. From that experience alone, I am going to share with you four stories of the various people that I encountered in those four hours. What I would like for you to do afterwards is to reflect on your past experiences if you have ever been to an adolescent center at your local hospital. Because my experience was probably far from what you think an adolescent center should be or is like today if you have not visited one in a while.

It all started after having heard and seen the second customer that came in for service, the situation became clear to me that what I was a witness to was a growing epidemic. One that is crippling our financial economic system, the future of our children, and a systematic attempt at setting up our children to fail flat on their faces. I was honestly shocked and dismayed to the severity of the situation at hand. This one incident had opened my eyes to a larger problem that has been spreading across America for more than 20 years.

The first story I want to tell you about this Adolescent Center relates to the behavior of this lady whom I thought was probably in her forties. The woman was at the center with her daughter seeking medical treatment. She, like most of the people that came to this department, had no sense of timeliness. They all were coming in late for their appointments or on the wrong day. This one woman was late and confused as to the time she was supposed to have been there. She was a familiar face. She had grown up in the system and now was actually raising her grandkids. She told Miss Logan, the staff member, that the young girl with her was her grandchild. All of her kids were all grown up and on their own, like a proud parent. She was taking care of one of her grandchildren now. A quiet, innocent young girl about 18 years of age. She was there for her regular checkup. She seem to have a good head on her shoulders and appeared quite smart compared to the other kids coming into the office.

As I looked at the grandmother who was all agitated and bewildered by now, it was clear she could not recall the time of her appointment. She was asking the grandchild to recall the date of her own appointment. Next, she could not seem to find her medical card on hand since the granddaughter was now on her insurance. She was a talker. Sharing with everyone what she has been up to with her life since it had been a while and her only concern was for the safety of her granddaughter.

Her biggest worry in life was about someone stealing her grandchild's iPod and robbing her for her money. It seemed that she was recently transferred from one good school to a bad one. So the grandmother was dealing with that. This was when my curiosity peeked and I asked Ms. Logan to find out her age.

It turned out that this young woman who came in was actually 50 years old, in good shape, and still lively. Ms. Logan and I were in disbelief when she told her how many grandchildren she really had. Apparently she had fourteen. She herself had four daughters and two sons.

A baffled Ms. Logan who had worked in the same department for over 30 years and had remembered her when she was a young adult too was shocked since she never knew that she had this many kids and was already in her 50s.

Regrettable, my concern for that young girl was that she does not whine up pregnant due to the type of environment she lived in. A far cry from what her grandmother felt was her biggest worry in life for this young 18 year old. I could only imagine the type of role models and support that 18 year old had in her life. Not to mention the continuous cycle of poverty she was likely trapped in. And here I was, at an adolescent center and seeing what she was exposed to probably her whole life.. Teenage mothers, teenage pregnancy, high school drop outs, and welfare recipients. Even this adolescent center that she frequented was no different from what her reality is. The odds against her are high that one day she will be in that same office too, having to worry about her own child getting jump for her MP3 player rather than the life she will soon bring into the world with no real guidance or support to break the cycle of a welfare mentality.

The second person that walked in to that office, catching my attention, was an Indian mother with her pregnant 18 year old daughter. The girl was due to give birth in late October or early November 2009. Here it was again; another sad story of a woman who came to America in search of a better life for her family, finding herself caught up in the American teenage trap of self-independence and defiance from their parents' upbringing. The young daughter apparently very shy and naïve had that plain look of cluelessness on her face as she knew her due date was soon approaching. Her life would never be the same again. And standing beside her was her mother. A woman with so many burdens to bear. A stranger to this foreign land, seeking a better future for her daughter, has no idea what lies ahead of her. What mountains she has to climb from this oppression and slave labor. She too kept a puzzled face not so different from her daughter's demeanor. Barely speaking English to understand what is truly going on in America and the youth of this generation. Yet she has to solely depend on her daughter's English to get through life. Maybe to her minimum wage job this is a better quality of life, the American Dream she had so much hoped for than the quality of life she left behind to come to America - with the hopes of a better future, if not for her, for her daughter and now her grandchild. The first American born citizen that will one day, with hope, fight for the equality and the respect their ancestors deserve as immigrants of the United States of America.

The third story that I came across that day was of two young happy teenagers coming in ready for their appointment. Well, at least the girlfriend was very excited to have the first pictures of her ultrasound exam. You should have seen the smile on her face. All happy and without a clue as to what they just have gotten themselves into. As if there was anything exciting to see two 16 year olds coming into an adolescent center for their baby checkup. Naïve about life and no financial means to even raise themselves let alone bring a child into this world. Meanwhile the boyfriend, who was not so thrilled, told Ms. Logan that he could not stand looking at the ultrasound pictures any more. That was all that she talked about.

Without hesitation, Ms. Logan and I looked at each other with the same comment in mind. "You will have 18 more years to look at your son in person." Sadly enough, with the stress that will follow him for the next twenty one years, this might be the most respectable gesture he might make before walking away from this young naïve 16 year old and leave her to raise that baby on her own. The odds of him sticking it out even to the birth seemed a long shot.

The fourth experience was actually a caller who was confused as to whom she was calling for and about. Ms. Logan had taken the call the second time this lady called seeking assistance for herself. The problem stemmed from the fact that she kept having her calls be rerouted back to the adolescent center for assistance when in fact that was not what she needed. After the third or fourth call back to the department, Ms. Logan tried to get to the bottom of the problem. She assured her that this was the adolescent center but she was calling for assistant about herself. Now her department could no longer help this young lady because she was past the age of 26 and was told to ask the switchboard for the "adult center" and not the adolescent center.

It was obvious to Ms. Logan and I that this young lady did not have the presence of mind to realize that she was passed the age of adolescence to still be taken care of in the same department she had gone to for the last few years.

After listening to the customer requests in that place each day, I know these employees must find some humor in what they do. The reality of it all can be a very depressing after thought. Certainly that was my train of thought to go through such an experience like this. In fact, I was so deeply disturbed by what I had seen that I reflected so much more as to the nature of this epidemic even as I dealt with my own children's choice to move out of the house at 19 years of age. The problem was clear.

Now to go back to the very beginning of this topic, I asked you to consider what you think of and what is your perception of a department named, adolescent center? To my surprise and very much to yours as well, I was appalled to see kids coming in there for themselves so they could get free services. My idea of an adolescent center has always been adult parents between the ages of 30 and 40 years of age coming into a hospital seeking care for their children. Not 16 to 21 year olds, as I saw walking in that day. And if you are thinking what I was thinking that day, I asked Ms. Logan if the cases that day had been unusual. She indicated that it had, in fact, been a typical day of who comes in for services. By now, it was clear to me who was behind this epidemic. The welfare systems have these kids so hooked into the idea of looking to be free from the disciplines of their household by getting out of the home as early as 18 years of age to get pregnant so that the system can provide them with housing and benefits.

Prior to this observation, I was oblivious to what was going on, even with my twins and their decision to move out with no comprehension of money, budgeting finances, let alone saving some for a rainy day, or more particularly, having the financial means to support themselves. In their minds, leaving home, moving out was a quick escape to adulthood-free from responsibilities, adult supervision, and parenting. They have been calculating and planning how they were going to move out ever since one of their friends got her own place. My twins' last ditch effort was to go shack up with their sister in a one bedroom apartment. Mind you I wrote this section in the summer of 2009 and by April of 2010, my wife had informed me that the girl with her own apartment was already pregnant. Moving forward to December of 2011, one of my twins had gotten pregnant and had a baby girl. And the cycle continues on.

I myself-probably no different than you are right now-was clueless to the world of babies having babies until I sat down with my father-in-law and discussed the situation. And here is what he told me was happening to this new generation of kids raising kids. Today's teenagers have already created their own network of communication with their friends via MySpace, Facebook, AIM, texting, or blogging online. They have so many ways of staying in touch that my Generation Xers and definitely our parents' generation did not have access to. By the time they are 18, they have already mapped out their whole strategy, it seems, as to how they are going to become independent. Their network of friends who have already experienced or have done it all by 21, have passed on the secret of independent living. They are being told that the best way to get your own place is to go ahead and get pregnant. Once that happens, they can apply for section 8 housing or assisted living for low income teens or pregnant teens. The welfare system and the government have been creating programs for these types of teenage mothers for years. Now the teenagers themselves have gotten wise on how to go about getting these types of assistance. Today the epidemic has gone way overboard to the point that these teenage mothers are no longer having one child but two or three at a time.

Stop for a minute and ask yourself this question: when was the last time you saw one of these teenage moms with only one child on the streets, train, or bus? It is a rare thing now a days. The system has already told them how much money they are being allowed to get with one child. So they have already figured out the new game. If they get two or more children, they will get more money. One lousy baby alone is not sufficient in covering all of their expenses. They still have to go clubbing, drinking, and wear the latest fashion in season. They all still have an image to uphold regardless if they're childless or pregnant. That baby was just a means to an end. A baby cramping up their life style was not part of the plan. The overall goal was to get that section 8 housing by any means necessary.

Let's not blame the kids alone for this problem because the parents play a big role in all this as well. However, we cannot forget the greatest contributor of them all, the welfare system and section 8 housing. As a responsible parent, my wife and I are planning on having our first child together. So of course I took a stroll near the baby section in one of these stores looking at the prices of baby strollers and carriages one day. I was shocked on how expensive these things are. At the same time it made me reflect on how expensive it is to have even one child let alone two.

As a concerned parent that is the big difference that separated us from these teenage moms. I don't have a welfare mentality to skip out of my responsibility as a parent. The teenagers of today seem to believe that our tax dollars is supposed to provide for them. Why not, we have an open checkbook policy it seems when they get pregnant. We come with open arms with support groups and support systems for them ready to aide in whatever shape necessary. Having worked at a hospital and a community center, I see children's coats, toys, baby strollers, carriages, and diapers for all stages of infancy. All of it free to these needy teenage moms who never put one thought into thinking, how am I going to provide for my child?

So why not take the *Free Lunch,* if it is offered to me. That is what they are thinking. "If you will provide it, I will gladly accept it and keep having more because your programs and systems will always be around each and every time I drop the ball as a teenage mom. You the taxpayer will fill all the necessities of life that I need to take care of my child. I don't have to take on any more responsibilities aside from wasting nine months of my life to have a fatherless child!" Honestly, it would not surprise me if that is really their mentality and thoughts.

To make matters worse, the systems provide these teenage moms with housing at a discount, with subsidies. I do not know what your city is like today but in Boston, new homes and high rise towers-(condos) are being built everywhere you turn around in the city. These teenagers are being told that they can easily move in to them if they fit the criteria: Pregnant, single moms, low income, etc. And as always they gladly abide by our adult rules and do as we say. So now you see these young teenage moms being put in newly constructed homes, single or double family occupancies. It is all part of this new gentrification project around the Boston community to bring folks closer to the city. But to give you the façade that says otherwise. I have been informed that some buildings even allow a few floors to be dedicated only to low income families just to say that the neighborhoods are diverse.

So what is my point? Well once again, our society is fooling our children to believing that they have arrived at success, at their highest level of achievement, and it is all a trap. Another attempt to entrap our children into thinking they do not need us as parents. That 18 years of age is good enough to stand on your own two feet and provide for your own family. What our children don't know is that even at 30, 40, 50, and sometimes at 60 years of age, parents are still struggling financially to provide for their loved ones. So what makes our teenagers think they are special or better than us old timers? The only difference is that they have been a captive audience in the system's games from day one and they never knew it. They have been conditioned to a state of mind.

For some of us, we have become so desensitized to the chaos around us that we can no longer see the problems in front of us. We can no longer see the end results of what we are doing economically to each other, to the rest of the world, to our children, and grandchildren's future. Most of us are simply living for the present only. There is no regards for this Earth, how we treat people, or the end results of our actions. We act as if we each live in our own world, dominated by our egos and nothing else matters but me, myself, & I.

It really amazes me that I can be surrounded by educated men and women but they don't believe that an economic collapse can occur. And the only difference that separates you and me is the perspective from which I see the future. Mainly from a business/entrepreneurial perspective as oppose to simply being an employee-minded person whose thoughts and actions have been conditioned to think a certain way.

Slow & Methodical

What you have just read is a small glimpse as to where we have come from since the days of the idiot box. The housing example is one of many if you do not pay close attention to, you will find yourself being conditioned as well.

I want you to look back on the gas crises of the past decade or so. We all have felt the pinch in our pockets each time we go to the pumps. And we will continue to deal with the cost of gas prices going up if we do not speak up about it. Do not wait until it is so outrageous that we cannot afford to go to the pumps anymore before we say something to our leaders. Let your voice be heard.

Unfortunately to your dismay, the gas companies have discovered a new trick that keeps you hush up at the pumps. The trick is very simple you see. Just look at when does the media cover the cost of gas prices going up? Isn't always after it has hit an all-time high? In fact it is the only time we all pay attention to it. We grunt and complain throughout the ordeal until the media brings it to light. But prior to that, they have sucked out a few billions of dollars out of your pocket in just a few weeks and you did not even feel it happening to your wallets.

The method by which the gas companies take money from you and deceive you is quite simple. They slowly increase the price of gas, by a few pennies every other day. After a while you do not even notice it. You say things like, "oh the gas prices went up a penny, must be the cost of inflation or the way things are" And you leave it be. You do not mind it but it slowly creeps up. Before you hear the anger and the news crew on TV speaking about it, it had gone up 15 to 30 cents on you without blinking an eye. All because your mind has been conditioned once again to accept your reality.

This is no different from the philosophy behind cooking a frog[xiii]. A frog uses its body temperature to adjust to the condition of its environment. Experiments have shown although frogs love water, they will not jump into boiling hot water. However put them in a bucket of cold water that is room temperature, they will indeed jump in. Furthermore if you slowly increase the temperature, it will adjust its own body temperature to match that of the boiling water. Eventually the frog is cooked without realizing that it was being prepared for dinner.

In network marketing (MLM) we use this phrase all the time. How do you cook a frog, "slow and easy"? We, as consumers are very much like frogs in the methods used to get us to buy more. Things like super-size it, special sale, everything must go, buy one-get one free, free shipping, and the favorite word that I hate is FREE, FREE, FREE. Things are described as "free" a lot online to get your contact information. The amazing thing about all of this is that a lot of companies do this to us every single day and the majority of folks do not get it. We are too blindsided by the commercials on the idiot box with all the sex and glamour.

Let's look at the phone companies for an example. One day I happened to see an Asian father showing his little boy how to play with his toy cellphone. As I watched them, all I could think of was the subliminal messages that we are sending to our children at such a young age and we don't see anything wrong with it. Stuff like that are little examples of how kids grow up demanding a cell phone from their parents as early as grammar school. Why? Because the system gets you to buy into the cell phone craze. Because parents see a toy cellphone as just a toy. What they have done instead is introduce your children to the function of a cellphone. And you as a parent do the rest by chatting, laughing, and carrying on in your conversations. Now guess who is watching you throughout their adolescent, your kids. They see what you do and they grow up wanting to do it to. The cellphone industry, meanwhile, is smiling to the bank because they know your kids are hooked on wanting a cellphone too. The sad thing is we accommodate our kid's request by getting them a family plan. Now the whole family has one, so we can all stay in touch. As if, in the 80s, we could not have done so without a cellphone. I never saw parents giving their child pagers so they could get in touch faster. In hindsight, that is marketing at its best and you as the parent play into the trap each time because your mind has been condition to accept that change.

I know that some of you right now are saying to yourself, well I never bought my kid a toy cellphone. Well if it is not the toy cellphone that you gave into, it is your personal cellphone that you just handed over to your child so you can keep them hush up. I see this all the time. We as parents start to use our personal cellphone as leverage when we are busy or distracted by another adult. To silence our children, we give into their demands-unconsciously and unaware of what we have just done again to them.

I will never forget the day I went to a Verizon store to get my phone repaired. Here was a family of 5 standing next to me about to upgrade the family plan so one of their children, who could not have been more than 10 years old, could get a new phone. Why! Is that cellphone really necessary? And that's where we start these traps of financial illiteracy. A child does not know one thing about managing a cellphone bill yet we give them one anyways. When they get older, they download ring tones, games etc. without any consideration for the cost. Even the bill sometimes does not even faze them.

The example of my adopted twin daughters provides a great look at the traps the system has setup for our children. By their seventeenth birthday, my wife was already arguing with them about the high cellphone bills that were coming in each month. Six months later my wife had enough. The bill eventually went as high as $1,000. That was the boiling point for my wife. The end result was to remove them from her contract. If you have kids, you know what they did next-get caught up in a contract of their own. Although I forewarned them not to get into a cellphone contract at their age and go with a prepaid phone provider, they chose to do what they wanted. Again, because of commercialism, they went with one of the sidekick carriers. They both got individual phones with a shared plan. Again, a parent reading this already knows what came next. Since they had their phones activated on the first month of their contract, they could not keep up with the payments each month. Their situation got so bad that it was like clockwork to expect every other month that their cellphones were shut off due to their inability to pay it. Last but not least, which brings me back to my point, their bill got so bad that they finally decided to ditch their cellphone provider to go with the newly popular Metro PCS that began spreading like wildfire all across the East Coast. All in all they have gone through four or six different providers, still not able to pay off any one of them. By the age of 19, bill collectors were already after them.

So why does this all matter? It does very much matter because of the decisions we allow our children to make at an early stage of life. We did not provide any discipline or value systems, any lessons on the responsibilities associated with owning a cellphone at a young age. We simply told them here you go. We are literally showing our children bad habits in spending by saying max out the cellphone minutes until I am fed up or blue in the face. Isn't that what we as parents are saying to our kids indirectly each time? We "forget" once again to teach the life principles and philosophies that come with owning a cellphone.

So let's go back to when my twins decided to "ditch" their cellphones. Like I have told my children at eighteen, you are no longer considered minors when you turn eighteen. The real world expects you to be and treats you like an adult. You are no longer considered a minor. Everything you sign or do has some sort of legal ramification going forward. This generation of children today don't get that ditching a cellphone is no longer like the games we play in school such as ditching class or ditching our dates. Their decision to just ditch their cellphones and go with another provider sets them up for failure. Today we all know how important having good credit is but our children don't know or even take the time to think about such things as credit. If anything, they will say, what is that? And that is one way the cycle starts again and the system goes back to the bank with a smile on their face, Cha-Ching! They got another one who will be paying high interest rates for life because they simply failed to learn some basic wealth principles of life. Like I have said all my life, it is the little things that matter most. Not really the big things. If we all did the little things that really matter the most, we would be okay when the big things came our way. In my daughters case, four years after life forced them on their own two feet, they could not get an apartment because of all the debt and bad credit they had accumulated - most of it before they turned twenty-one.

One way to avoid this entire headache is to simply start your kids off with a prepaid cellphone. My first cellphone was prepaid. Actually, back then you either had a prepaid phone or a hefty cellphone contract that would have cost you an arm and a leg as a down payment. A prepaid cellphone reinforces all the disciplines that you want your child to pick up in their adolescent. If you are going to give your child a cellphone at that age, you should put restrictions on them. It is no different if you were going to limit the internet usage on the computer for them. This method is used to protect your children from predators online, child-pornography, rapist, molesters, and the online social networks. They are too young to be exposed to these things. Yet we do not deem it necessary to do the same to our children when it comes to their cellphone usage. As of 2010, a cellphone is not just a cellphone any more. Your phone is now an extension or a replacement of your computer or laptop these days. Namely look at the iPhone, the Android, and the Google phones. They all share similar functions such as music, texting, email, wireless internet, video streaming, DVD like quality movies, apps, and more. What's important to know about the latest phones today is not necessarily all the cool features they all have but rather, the hidden fees and charges attached to them. All the features I have listed so far require either a data plan or a service fee for usage on top of your regular phone plan. Again another financial cost to you the parent who wants to reassure your child is safe when they are not with you. Unfortunately what you have created for yourself is a financial nightmare as your child racks up the cost of using all of those features every month. Leaving you to foot the bill each month. As someone once said to me, giving your child a prepaid phone forces them to learn how to manage their minutes. It also limits the lack of judgment early on that the phone is not something you just chat and have fun with but that there are costs associated with its usage. A young kid does not get it like an adolescent does but you the parent don't seem to get it either. You are setting your children into a financial mess, which can be avoided with a limited functioning prepaid cellphone. When they prove to be responsible, then upgrade them to the fancier cellphones.

The burden of a cellphone bill has nothing to do with minutes being used. That was the old days when we all were worried about how many minutes we had left. With the options of Skype for your phone, unlimited minutes, and shared family plans, worrying about your minutes running out should be the last thing on your mind.

Today's cellphone bills have everything to do with the data plan that they offer. Do not get fooled by the word games that the phone industry plays on uneducated consumers. Free and unlimited data plans are being used a lot as catch phrases to deceive consumers. We have been educated enough in school to know what the word "unlimited" means but to the phone companies they have a new redefine meaning. To them "unlimited" means an estimated amount of usage for the average consumer. Therefore once you go over the average unlimited usage, you find yourself with a ridiculous phone bill.

Sprint, in 2012, has been the only company that has declared themselves to be a true unlimited data provider. The only reason you and your child have not experienced this thus far is that you all have not pass the undisclosed limit. But do not be quick to breathe a sigh of relief. Verizon has come up with new commercials that encourages our youth to start streaming their concerts and parties to their friends via their new 4G cellphones. In actuality, they are encouraging our youth to get into the habit of downloading huge amounts of data, which can lead to an exuberant amount of dollars in overage charges.

On April 2010, the Boston Globe[xiv] reported that Verizon charged a family $18,000 for a cellphone bill. It seems as though their 20 year old son at the time was using his family plan cellphone as a modem uplink to surf the internet on his laptop. He presumed that the 30 day free downloads that they had gotten after upgrading their phone plans was unlimited. Again no financial knowledge on how much a phone plan cost but parents are carelessly signing up for these family plans that they think are unlimited.

If you thought this was bad, countries like Sweden makes Verizon's $18,000 charge look like child's play in comparison. The cellphone industry and the banks out there are finding creative ways to lure young adults between the ages of eighteen and twenty-five, who want to text on their cellphone. The banks in Sweden are allowing young teens to take out text loans or rather SMS loans from the banks so they can text their friends. Since the inception of this new idea in mid-March of 2006, teens are getting into huge debt because they cannot pay the high interest costs on these texting loans. It has gotten so bad that by 2007, it was reported that a debt recovery agency by the name of Kronofogden out of Sweden was the first to be given the task in collecting over 20,000 such loans. Within 15 minutes or less, you can take out a loan via your cellphone of course. There is no contract or signature needed. All you have to do is request it. The target market has been mainly teenagers and low income teens. They are being bombarded with these fast cash loans via the public transportation systems, buses, on the streets, newspapers, and television ads. All in all enticing them to go ahead and borrow. Borrow with no restrictions or limitations. Now it is becoming an epidemic all over Sweden. Today you can also find text lenders in Estonia, the Netherlands, and Finland doing the same thing.

What a sad way to start your kids off in debt while still in elementary school and in high school. Parents please don't get complacent or gullible in thinking that the methods businesses use to market to our children is harmless. Take some time to watch Nickelodeon, SpongeBob Square Pants, and the Disney Channel, to name a few, with your kids. It's more than just cartoons they are watching. You will be surprised at what you see subliminally. And we have not even scratched the surface of what companies are doing to market to your children let alone keeping your best interest in mind as an adult. We'll talk about those things in chapter nine.

WHAT IS YOUR SLAVESHIP?

As each generation evolves and new technology is created, humanity seems to get lazier and lazier. On March 10th, 2010, I saw something that caught my attention which is a perfect place to start this chapter. One morning I saw a lady that was about to get on our slaveship for work and I happened to notice what she was doing. Instead of picking up the small bag with wheels she had with her, she dragged it on a full bus. As great as it is to see the revitalization of an old industry such as they did with the luggage industry by putting a new spin on it, all it did was create a new problem. I have even watched little kids going to school, dragging their school bags on wheels. To you it may not be much, but as an observer of the world, it's really a form of dumbing down America by way of laziness. Today you find kids whining when you ask them to simply pick up their school bags instead of wheeling it around. It sure brings a new meaning to the concept of "stop dragging your bag around" today. As these kids grow up to become adults, it's just another thing they can't fathom doing—consequently making them even lazier than ever before.

Most of the kids that I see on my slaveship cannot even take a second to pay attention to the world around them. Their world is filled with distractions. Malcolm Gladwell made the same observation in, "*The Tipping Point*", about sound and music. Scientists have spent decades doing research and have mastered subliminal messaging to us via the music we listen to. Let's not pretend that the systems have never used that technology on us. I have witnessed it a lot while riding on my public slaveships. I have seen how much our children have become dumb down to the world around them, just by listening to certain music on a daily basis. I have even notice adults doing the same thing because of this fad over iPods and MP3 music players. The system wins every time music is being blasted in their ear drums. Many times it is so loud that you can hear the music playing just by sitting or standing next to them. They are not observing what's around them or seeing what the system is doing to them. If only they took the time, they would see that there is a better quality of life than the one being offered to their generation.

As much as Apple has revived its image to not just being known as a computer base company, it has indirectly become the leader of an industry that has made people clueless and inattentive of their environment. I use the words "slaveship" to help you see how not so far off your life has been from working in an invincible shackles for 30 to 40 years of your life without ever knowing it. I purposely put the two words together to deceive you since your mind will separate them as two separate words that should not be put together. Furthermore your eyes might have even played tricks on you to thinking it is one word. Eventually your brain will accept it as what it is. Likewise your job has made you unconsciously unaware that your place of employment is that ship that you go into each week day to make a living but you are indeed the slave that works there. It is hard for us to conceive this notion as a fact but I guarantee you, you will understand how that can be after reading this chapter.

Dateline NBC[xv] has a TV show called, *"Did You See That?"* The show looks at how easy it is to deceive our eyes when we are looking at something right in front of us. We live in a world so detached from everything that we could not even be a credible witness to an accident due to our cellphones, our tablets, handheld video games, or iPods entertaining us. Likewise I want you to understand how your job itself continues to dumb you down indirectly, without consciousness. Therefore making you slave to your job.

When I am on my slaveship I am always doing one of three things: observing, reading, or reflecting. You would be surprised at the amount of things you can pick up along the way about human behavior. All of us have ridden in one during the course of our career to work so we can do the 40/40/40 plan each week with a promise of a golden key at the end of it all. I am going to share with you my observations and experiences of what I see and hear on the trains and buses that have become our slaveships to work.

- I have seen grown adults getting out of their house before 5:30AM to catch their bus in time for work. A scary thing for women who are in the nursing field since hospitals are open 24-7.

- I have watched people tired and beat down by the type of jobs they do. I have seen people stand for eight or more hours at work, having to come home to a family that needs their attention.

- I have seen men and women stuck in traffic averaging one hour or more each way, only to do it again the next day because they live an hour away.

- I have watched groups of four teenagers on the train with a baby on one hand and a carriage on the other, ready to go to school.

- I have watched other teenage moms during the summer times get off the train, prostituting their new born babies in exchange for their freedom. Others as young as twelve years old have already put away their Barbie dolls so that they can carry a real live one of their own.

- I have even listened to the conversation of today's youth. At times, I hardly hear anything but the clashing noise of a cellphone keypad being over worked.

- When it comes to adults, I hear the same complaints over and over again about that promotion they did not get. That department or company that is laying off people. Worries about their 401K, the stock market, or their college bound kids.

There were other days that I did not have to hear anyone but just reflect on the life of a middle age man like on January of 2010 as I saw him sit down on the train ride home. You could tell that he was a hardworking man in his fifties who made a living as a painter. Riding the train hunched over from a long work week. Deep in self-reflection probable about his life and whether or not he will be able to retire or is he destine to live his golden years working until his death since he really does not have much to show for it. The stain of spilled paint stuck on his paints, shoes, and hands are the only things he has left to show for his hard work today, this week, this month, this year. The memories are all wrapped up as a single choice made a long time ago destined to be repeated over and over again each day until his maker calls him home. In the end, all he has to show for what he lived for was a lousy paycheck that determined his future every day. His nights are probably spent in bed resting a bad back.

One of the things that I have noticed about working a 9-to-5 is that it really does not teach you to be independent of your boss or manager. Everything that requires a decision to be made has to come from someone senior to you. Over time, all you have done is make yourself obsolete, unable to think outside the box. You have voluntarily conditioned your mind not to think critically. You have refused to become your own problem solver.

I have watched how often people do that being in the IT field. Simple things that could have been resolved in a matter of minutes, if they had made an effort to do so would not cause delays or cost a company hours or days to fix. And if you work in a union or government job, you can forget about it. You will find enough red tape to go around the Earth to the moon twice. I believe in some places it is even illegal for you to expect one person to do one task and finish the second part to that task. Nope, another union employee must come in and finish the second part, else you are taking away someone else's job.

It is unfortunate that most employees lack the foresight to see problems and create solutions outside the box of their 9–to-5 job requirements. There is also an unspoken rule that because management is the one being paid the big bucks, they are the ones who are supposed to do all the thinking. Average employees are not given the privilege to think on the job. If you are wondering whether or not that description fits you at your job, ask yourself this question: When a decision has to be made or a customer request something outside of the norm, can you make that decision yourself or must you use the words, "I must speak to my manager about that" or "I cannot make that change without consulting my manager first."

Anyway you put it, if you alone cannot make a decision without having to worry about the consequences of that decision, then you are not allowed to think for yourself. Someone of a higher authority must think for you regardless if you know the answer, else it will be seen as going over your manager's head.

So when I say your job dumbs you down, I mean that it is unconsciously done every day and you hardly notice the difference. That is one reason why you need to become an entrepreneur, to use your creative genius to think outside the box.

As entrepreneurs, 90% of our brain power is used to think outside that box that society puts you in. Being an entrepreneur forces you to think outside the box and make decisions constantly. In hindsight, it also expands our mind, our sense of awareness, and the vision to plan ahead in life. Being a problem solver also allows you to create a vision of tomorrow through business development.

What's the difference?

An apple is an apple just like an orange is still an orange; put together they are called fruits.

A ship filled with cargo is still a ship. A train or a bus filled with people is still a train or a bus. But when put together they are forms of transportation that delivers goods.

A corporate office filled with cubicles and executive offices awaiting butts in seats to operate a company is still a building.

However, if you live in these tough economic times, they are all forms of slaveships that take you to and from work every week without questioning the status quo.

So really what is the difference between what you do now and slavery? I have been working on a poem entitled, *"On My Slaveship I Go."* I want you to listen to the words carefully and see the comparisons that I made as I ride my train slaveship to work.

All I see staring at me while passing by is a commuter train full of people with little windows to look through. In my mind's eyes, all I see is the reflection of true slave ships from the 18th and 19th century. The only difference is that these ships were at sea and today they are on wheels or train tracks. They are crowded with volunteer slaves with an ID badge attached to their waste line. Back then slaves had their shackles tied to their arms and feet. Today's slaves have new and improved shackles that allow them to perform their work more efficiently so that their old chains do not interfere with their computer keyboard.

Like most people, I have worked in a highly secured environment that required that I wear an ID badge. We all need to wear them for security. You can understand their purpose but as an entrepreneurial-minded individual, you have to remove them as fast as you can after your shift ends. They are part of your slave gear.

I watch people after work sometimes still wearing their IDs. One thing is for sure, these employees are exposing themselves to ID theft but, what is more obvious, is that they are still acting the role of a captive slave. These are the people whose subconscious are really stuck on the job; it does not make a difference to them.

Unless you have some business sense, you won't quite understand what I am saying. Your job may own you for those eight hours but entrepreneurs never let the job own their mind as well. That's why we make sure to leave the company cell phone and pager in the office. We keep even the company email off at the office when it is time to check out. For me it is like a check in and check out daily service. When you are at home working on your business, the work email is not even checked at all. Your focus is entirely on your business at that time; 100% of your attention needs to be spent on your business. No distractions or chores for your family or taking care of the kids, or doing errands. When you are at home or your place for doing your business, make it be all that you do for that period of time. There is no in between. Your job would never allow you to do your personal business on company time. So why not extend the same respect to your own business; that same respect that you give your boss five days a week? It is the least you can do for yourself and your family's future.

Our society has been moving away from physical labor and more towards intellectual labor as a valuable asset to have in the near future as robots begin doing more of the heavy lifting for us. Within the next sixty years or by the start of the 22nd century, we will be moving towards an enlightenment age for a lack of a better word or the illumination of the mind, where any form of physical labor will be seen as miniscule work or low wage jobs that no one wants to do anymore. These types of workers will be seen as those who do not possess the intellectual capacity to have a high paying job.

What does it matter to you, you may say because you will not live to see one hundred years? Well your children will. And if you want to move forward in the right direction, you better start teaching them the ways of the future. Do not let your family get stuck in 20th century thinking, hoping to survive in a 21st century world with technology.

Even though we are years away from this becoming a reality in your life today, we are currently in the initial stages of what is to come fifty to one hundred years from now. So the signs are there as we start the second decade into the 21st century. The science fiction of tomorrow just happens to be in the formulation stage. One thing for sure, technology moves real fast. I know. I live it every day.

So if you are the other half of the working class who never pay attention while at their job as to what is going on with the rest of the country. Keep putting your head down and see how long you will be at that job. Often people watch the news, get a little concern but eventually they go back to work while ignoring the writing on the wall. As if the issues facing America's unemployed, baby boomers, and other societal problems really do not concern them because they have a safe secure job with benefits. Their company is healthy, they have enough saved up in the bank, their pension or 401(K) is intact. All of these assumptions are why people are finding themselves dipping into their retirement income, their savings, or 401(K) plan before reaching retirement age. Everyone seems to be living only for today and tomorrow's problems will be dealt with, of course tomorrow. There is no future planning or goal setting in middleclass

American households any more. Our mindset is whatever comes our way will be dealt with at that time. Who cares about the future! Hence is the reason why we are where we are in America today, at the end of the road figuratively speaking of course.

Over the years working in the E quadrant of life, I have seen the end results of what being an employee-minded person does to one's soul and the ability to think outside the box. Most of us are doing the same mundane task each week and hardly pay attention to anything outside of the norm. As time goes on, we lose our ability to make common sense decisions and look more like zombies pushing a button. We start buying into these catch phrases or nuances like - I cannot wait till hump day, meaning Wednesday. As if the week is really going to go by any faster. We all start complaining come Sunday about Monday. Monday is basically drag day. We are all dragging our feet in the office. Friday is called, TGIF… "Thank God it's Friday."

Let's take a look at how each one of these groups of people attempt to relieve their stress or cope with the daily grind.

The Working Class:

Some of us work hard five to six days a week so we can get that paycheck come Friday. And many just spend it up when they get it. There are some that just go out and gamble it all away at the liquor store, the strip club, the night club, or the shopping mall. Others cannot wait until Friday comes so they can start parting all weekend long. Hence the reason they call it TGIF. For others, it is a chance to finally put their feet up and stay in the bed and rest throughout the weekend. Some of us have already made plans for the weekend and cannot wait. Whether it is a date or a great weekend getaway planned, we all seem to be living it up only for the weekends to come so we can enjoy it and make those two days off last as long as possible.

College/University Students:

It is not that different for college students because they have their own nuances too. It's just much simpler than those in the real world. Monday through Wednesday nights school work. Thursday through Saturday nights starts off the club/party scene. Rest on Sunday mornings, study, and do homework Sunday nights. That was the college life I was surrounded by.

For those who never lived on campus, it really is not that different from the working class because there is always a house party going on during the weekends. Just listen to the loud music or look for the trails of beer cans laid out all over the bushes and street corners.

Church Folks:

I am a good ole church boy. I was raised and brought up in the Catholic Church. But most importantly, I have allowed myself to be exposed to a variety of religions since I was a child. All in all I see it all too often and it is especially true with Baptist and Pentecostal churches. People are in tears crying out to the Lord in pain because they are suffering. To you, they might appear to be filled with the Holy Spirit but to me it's all about releasing the pain. Some even get hysterical, shouting out in prayer, and jumping off their feet. Yet for most of them, they don't know why they are in so much pain. They don't understand that although they may be free to roam the land, there is still an invisible slave chain around their necks, arms, and legs. We cannot see all the invisible shackles that man has put around us to keep us enslaved but I promise you they are there. The poor and middle class are suffering because the same people they honor and respect at their jobs are the ones who have put these shackles on them. Some of them are blinded by their faith to see that they are in a prison camp.

From time to time, I look at these folks who go to church on Sundays in a different light. I watch these folks who are struggling every day. They cannot wait to get to church and pray for a better day. Church, to them, has become their safe haven away from their worries. It is the one place they can cry out to God. I could never understand these people who start shouting out, dancing all over the place. But to some extent I really do because I see it all the time. For some it is the only security they have. Church is the only thing that makes sense of the ever changing world around them. Church is really their bandage for what they have to deal with five to six days a week, 9-to-5. Sometimes it is a double shift or 60 to 80 hours a week work schedule just to maintain and keep what they have.

To me the bandage is their peace and tranquility for having to deal with a job that they don't like, a boss who is a double S.O.B or at times clueless to what they should be doing as a boss, dealing with a working environment that is all politics or cut throat, dealing with colleagues that you hardly care to associate with but you have no choice but to work with them. Some of them have no class, and are disrespectful, gossipers. Some have big egos, and are back stabbers, etc. The list goes on and on.

Nevertheless, they struggle with all these stresses and prepare mentally to go to work on Monday. And some of us still claim to love their jobs. In hindsight some may love their job but if you ask them about their pay, it is usually a different story. In most cases, you either love what you do but don't get paid well or you are paid well but you do not love what you do. At the end of the day, it is all too depressing to reflect on it. So all they can do is cry out and ask God for a better day, a better life, a better future.

Today, churches are overcrowded with folks looking for a prayer, a good word to motivate them for Monday. Through my eyes, I see churches becoming more of a hideaway place before the week starts, another safe house, or a resting place to make it through the week. These occurrences are becoming too common in big cities and you now see churches extending their services. My church, for example, created an additional service mid-week and added a third service on Sunday.

As each year gets harder and harder, it's becoming obvious that some of us just cannot wait until Sundays any more to be refilled in the word. A refresher is so needed due to the struggles and stresses that we face each day at our jobs. And then there are those who are just praying, how are they going to make it through another week Lord? Being renewed by the word of God during the week keeps them holding on until Sunday comes. Our faith is then restored by Sunday's service through a good word from the Bible. But at the end of the day, we find ourselves preparing mentally to repeat the same cycle again.

To sum it all up, we spend our whole life coming into this world as a baby, so that someone can take care of us into our teenage years where we fight so much for our freedom; then we grow up to adulthood seeking our independence only to reach old age just to go back and be dependent on someone else to take care of us-simply because we failed to plan for our final years to retirement. Does that make any sense at all? But that is the cycle of the life we choose to live. When I hear or see stories like these, I have to ask you, the hard working dedicated employee, the million dollar question, is your job an asset to your future? You be the judge as you read the next sub-chapter.

IS YOUR JOB AN ASSET OR A LIABILITY?

I know those who are not business minded may be a bit confused by the question I have set as the title here - is your job an asset or a liability? The phrase is commonly used to reference how well you understand real estate. It is one of the most important questions that Kiyosaki poses through many of his real estate books. It may sound stupid since we normally do not think of our jobs as an asset. We more or less think, when we buy a house, that it is an asset. Contrary to popular belief, though, your house is not an asset. The majority of home owners today actually own a liability. The classification of your house is simply determined by your level of financial literacy to know the difference. Whether or not you want to accept the truth, your house is a business. How you treat it is what determines if you bought an asset or a liability. Let's not worry about it right now because understand where you are at your job is of the upmost importance to your future.

Back in the 1970s and 1980s, corporate America use to think of you as an asset to the company, once you have been there a number of years. You were fresh out of college, bright, naïve about the world, and eager to make a good impression at your new job. Those were the good old days when you brought some value to a company.

In the 21st century, that really does not matter. You are an expendable commodity that can be replaced as fast as you came into the door.

Upper management sees you more of a liability than an asset to a company. It is especially true if you have been at your job for thirty plus years and have never gotten laid off. You have been a loyal employee for all of those years. But the words "loyal employee" does not mean you are an asset to your company. As a matter a fact, you are probably their biggest liability to date; and they can't wait to get rid of you.

Let me explain how you are a liability. Although you may not think like a corporate executive, their job is to measure risk and the liabilities of the company. They carry out the long term goals of the company. And at any time, you can be seen as a liability vs an asset to the company you work for. A former insurance agent once told me that the average employee is worth up to a $100,000 in liabilities.

Here are the things that they worry about when your number comes up. Because you have been a committed employee for all these years, you have built up too much vacation and sick time. You are probably at the maximum allowed in your pay grade and all other available benefits to you. You might have a legacy pension plan that they must honor. Last but not least, your salary is too high for what they can pay two people to do today or automate via a computer.

Let me stop here for a minute to remind you about that "joke" of a vacation that we wait for. We all know that we need a vacation. But why is it that when you take one so you can get away from the day to day stresses of your job, what ends up happening is that you come back to work with twice the work load you had before you left and hundreds of emails that you have to play catch up to? And the reason you feel that way is that there is no one else available but for you to do it.

A matter of fact, today you can easily find yourself doing two to three people's jobs just to keep that one job of yours. So you end up even more stressed out than before. So what's the point of a vacation when nothing changes? We just get back to the same grind or as Kiyosaki would put it, "the same rat race" as before. Now you need a vacation from the vacation that you took. Maybe it is just another cover up from the pain and reality that we are trying to escape from.

Job Security

In 2010, as the economy was slowly recovering, I began to hear a new word being used frequently in the job market. The word was "job security" and it was supposed to explain why they cut staff and now forced you the employee to do the work of two or three people and claim that it is job security. I almost wanted to laugh at my boss when I was sitting in his office one day and I shared with him how stressful it has been because we were under staffed and over worked. His only response was "it means job security" for keeping busy. To my colleagues it was their new catch phrase and the culture of corporate America.

Everywhere I worked I heard employees using that phrase as if there is such a thing as job security any more. Corporate America had made every hard working American dependent on their job for survival. We are so dependent that we claim it to be job security as oppose to teaching employees to be self-efficient, self-reliant, and be more conservative of resources on the job. Everyone in corporate America seems to be doing the bare minimum today so they can keep their jobs. I guess that is why they only pay you just enough so that you don't quit. And you really put forth enough effort so you don't get fired.

In my case, as a technician, each time someone did not understand something about how to repair or resolve a technical issue, it became job security for the staff members. When you hear words like that spoken amongst your colleagues in the office, know that they only have one mind set, the one that only thinks like a typical employee.

Let me remind all of you who are gainfully employed what job security really is. Your job security is only as good so long you do not outlive your usefulness. Because at any given point in time, you will be cut, given the pink slip, outsourced, replaced by a computer program, come to the end of your contract, or laid off. So no matter how you want to put it, your "job security" has an expiration date attach to your name. Now that you are no longer needed in the workforce corporate America has a new definition for you. It's called "over qualified" or you "have too much experience." How funny how times have changed when one generation ago, that was what companies wanted. Today it is all about cheap labor. A job today is as equivalent to those being shipped overseas for lower income workers.

I know some of you have been hard at work trying to make ends meet but had you stop for a moment to breath and see the world for what it is today, you would have notice a few things. Namely that your replacement[xvi] is young children, teenagers, or young adults fresh out of college. In exchange for your early retirement or unemployment benefits, they are filling up your old office. They are no longer just working at McDonald's or at a cell phone company retail location. They are the new faces of corporate America. They are getting younger and younger each time you go to the store. McDonalds is no longer their chosen place of work. They are working at professional jobs, businesses, and your local grocery stores-not as regular clerks but as managers and supervisors. Who is really working at McDonald's is you at 50 or 60 years of age as a greeter or clerk. The Wal-Mart's of the world loves your kind and so do the restaurant industry, and the shopping mall security jobs. And one of the main reasons why this is happening to you is that this new generation is having kids so young.

As a baby boomer, you are being forced out of the workforce by your grandchildren. As I have stated in previous chapters already, they want to be adults and have kids, and now they need to provide for them. So employers and our government welcomes them with open arms and push you off to the side. Why? Simply because they do not carry the same liabilities that you care about. Their babies are their biggest liability to come but with a twenty year delay. So our systems really do not care for now about dealing with them because they have the same plans for those parents too. You must remember that this new generation of kids do not care about owning a house, 401K, pension, retirement, healthcare, etc. or their future just yet. They believe that they still have time. I will explain more in later chapters and help you further understand why this all relates to entrepreneurship.

Well, by now you might be thinking of switching fields to find something more secure or you might possibly be thinking that folks like me in the IT field will always have job security because everything will be computerized. Well, that could not be further from the truth. Although we are indeed moving towards a technological driven world, it does not always mean everybody in technology will be safe from having their jobs eliminated. On the contrary, anyone who does any form of physical labor is in danger, including desktop support and field services. Everything if possible, will become automated from the push of a button, a key stroke, a command, or a remote control. And those who managed, operated, or monitored such machinery will eventually find their job obsolete in some form or another. If you don't believe me, just let time pass and your children will live to see it. It is already happening in 2013. President Obama has call for new engineers, new technology, and alternative fuel energy to be developed to power these new ideas. These are the coded messages being disseminated on your idiot box, social media, or newspapers that are calling for these new innovations to be developed by your future children and grandchildren.

This is why I laugh at myself sometimes for believing at one point in time that I would not be eliminated from my job one day because I am in IT. To date, I have been laid off at least five times since 9/11 in my journey to entrepreneurship. Therefore, I have been watching how technology is slowly but surely planning my extinction. But before I go into details, I want to tell you the main reason why I got into the IT field.

As a kid growing up in America, I fell in love with technology. I always found technology fascinating. In high school, I spent countless hours in a small Apple Computer lab after school, playing video games. The curiosity of computer games lead me wanting to understand how do I copy software; which led to me wanting to know how the inside of a computer works; which led me to wanting to take a computer apart to learn how to fix it. The journey all together led me to fall in love with the IT field. However that was not the only reason I fell in love with the IT field.

As a kid, I was always a visionary. In middle school, I had envisioned a future where I could work from home and raise my children without ever worrying about a 9-to-5 commute. Now this was the late 80s and early 90s. This type of technology was not even created yet. No one had even heard of the world wide web yet. If anything a global telecommunication network was the fantasy of all nerds at the time. The idea was not even popular. Computers were not even affordable and they were far from being a household appliance for the average home owner. I did not even own a computer at home. My middle school had ancient computers that stood in the back collecting dust because no one used them. I never even touched one but only stared at them. It was not until I got into high school that I got a chance to even touch a computer. It was after having put in my 10,000 hours[xvii] as Malcolm Gladwell puts it in his book that I started seeing the computer industry as a vehicle with which I can accomplish a childhood fantasy. I never knew how I was going to get there but the thought stayed with me throughout my teenage years. As I got older, I saw the importance of family and why being a stay at home dad was important to me. It would take four more years while in college to build a solid desire to want to own my own business.

When I was young, entrepreneurship was in me but the passion was not strong until I finished school in 1999 and began to venture off into the real world. Until then, I never heard of the word "entrepreneur" nor could I even spell the word right. All I knew was that I wanted to be in business for myself. Thus "business" was the only word that I knew. Ever since that childhood vision I have been building and preparing for the day I can really walk away from my J.O.B and never look back.

As I got older and continued building on my computer skills, I was beginning to recognize that the very technology that I had come to love would eventually make me, the technician, obsolete one day. I was starting to become more and more aware of how the industry was changing due to improvements in technology. So I started working on my plan B in life. Today, my fears and concerns could not be more relevant than when I hear these words: "Server Farms, Thin Clients, RDP, and solid state devices." If you are not in the IT field then these words might not mean much to you but if you are, then you should be very scared or working harder on your plan B than you do studying to get another IT certification by Microsoft, Apple, or Dell.

Let me explain what these words mean and why they are scary words for any field technician or IT specialist. A server farm is a more secure place, where companies can house their servers via an independent company warehouse such as in a storage facility. It is a centralized place where cost is reduced and overhead expenses in maintaining a company's server in-house are eliminated. The tragedy of 9/11 created a massive shift in the industry as to why any one company should house their server in-house where one hundred percent failure rate can be expected if faced with another terrorist attack. It eliminates the need for an in-house staff to support and maintain it. It is accessible through a virtual private network (VPN) tunnel if needs be. And they manage your servers for you. Today we call that cloud computing or cloud storage.

Thin Clients are small compact devices that function without a physical hard drive inside. They are light weight and cost-efficient compared to computers, which have a short shelf life. It creates a virtual session where all your programs are stored and accessible via a server. All data are stored in a centralized location on the server. No software needed to be installed. It is self-managed and easily replaceable. Aside from your cellphone or a tablet, this one item alone has already replaced the need for office computers.

RDP stands for Remote Desktop Protocol. It is a simply software that allows a user to connect to a computer running Microsoft Terminal Services on mostly any platform. All that is needed to run this program is a virtual server somewhere across the world to run it and a personal computer of any kind. It removes the need for a support staff and reduces the cost of unnecessary equipment purchase and maintenance. Last and most important to the decline of technicians is the invention of a solid state device or mother board. This device allows all of the components (chips) of a computer to be embedded into one solid board. In other words, there are no moving parts at all. So if one part breaks, malfunctions, or needs repairing, the whole thing is replaced. There is no need for troubleshooting or spending countless hours shipping parts, installing, or repairing anything because everything function as one solid state device. This new style of computing can be found in Apple's entire line of hardware and computers today.

To restate my point, there is no such thing as job security in any industry, including IT. If you were to reread the above paragraph again, you will see that there is no human element to all of these new and improve technological advancements that I have defined. All you do is set them up once and they are set up, they are all self-managed and sufficient. There is less of a need for a field technician like myself today because computers are less complicated and cost-effective to either replace it, support it on your own, or get online support. It no longer takes a genius to have a personal computer at home anymore.

Everything is plug-and-play just like a flash drive is. You and I no longer need a dictionary of terminology or a dummies book to figure out what is wrong with a computer.

So if you were in my shoes, why would you keep living in a pipe dream, believing that you will not become obsolete yourself within the next ten years? Hence my only question to you is this. For those who are currently working a 9-to-5 job or thinking about going into business for yourself for the first time, I want you to think about this question carefully? How can you ignore the signs on the wall for your job? You are being told each day about your future at that company and of your so call "job security" that you might have bought into for so long? No matter how you look at it, the thought is bleak. There is no happy ending for you in retirement heaven; there is no such thing.

Government Jobs

So what about your government jobs? Maybe you are not getting my point. It really does not matter what the job is. If you are an employee or do not own that building when you walk in it, you are in danger, at risk of being obsolete one day, of being laid off, regardless of where you work. I know, I know, some of you are still in disbelief because it is the government. They have money right? They are secure right? Yes, very secure in what is in it for them and not you the employee. You know something, I was once like you. I grew up probably like you believing in the same lies that our parents told us.

For years, we've been told that the best jobs are government jobs. They all have the best benefits, the best pay, and the best retirement package you could ever ask for. Maybe you even spent time trying to get one of those government jobs to secure your financial future. Maybe you have been, trying to find that hook up to get you in the door. That is usually how many of you got your government job. And I am sorry to say, been there, done that, and got the T-shirt.

Although I was never someone who was gun-hoe about getting one of those governmental jobs, I did manage to get one by accident when I worked in Springfield, MA.

Yes, I can speak from experience, you do get all the perks of vacation time, and sick leave that we have all heard about. A matter of fact my wife even has a government job today. So I do have the inside scoop of what it is really like.

The reason why I call them lies is because they are also traps or liabilities to your financial future. If you are serious about becoming an entrepreneur or a business owner a government job is really the last thing you want because of those perks. If I were to try and describe what a government job is or does to someone like you, who has plans to become an entrepreneur, then I would say government jobs are like vampires sucking the life out of you.

Having all of those perks, many people have given up on their dreams. The security of all of those great benefits is too alluring to walk away from. It takes a lot of will power to do it.

After a year and a half working for the City of Springfield, I found it very hard to let go. It was a power struggle for me, even as a young man knowing what I was going to give up to pursue my dreams. If it was not for God and the belief that I had a bigger purpose in life, I would have stayed behind and given up on all of my dreams and aspirations of becoming an entrepreneur. And that is why I honestly tell people that I hate government jobs.

If you think about it, there is not too much you have to do to keep your job. You get raise after raise, union benefit after union benefit. Your boss may even deny you a departmental raise but it really does not matter because if City Hall is giving out a raise, everyone else gets one too.

In fact, you can be a lousy employee working for the government. It does not matter because you can hide under the radar or fight back with the help of your union rep. As everyone knows, it is hard for you to lose your government job. My wife has shared with me a lot of stories of people who, if they had been in the private sector, would have lost their jobs in a heartbeat.

Still, there are some drawbacks that make a government jobs no safer positions within corporate America. Unfortunately, some of those drawbacks are more dangerous than you could ever imagine, being at your place of employment, feeling so safe and secure with all those benefits. I will talk about some of them in later chapters but will focus on a few in this chapter.

If you think about those words "safe and secure", one could easily imagine the safest place and secured place on earth being a prison cell. And that is what maximum security feels like if you have ever been in prison.

If you are hiding behind your government job, thinking it is the safest place to be in this economy, I want to be the first one to tell you that nothing could be further from the truth. And it all has to do with the state of the economy.

As it continues to get worse, your retirement is at stake. I know you believe that it is guaranteed but it is not; not when the government itself is broke. They cannot pay baby boomers back because the systems have spent the money or in legal terms, they have borrowed the money. They have borrowed it, in fact, to pay off old debts or pet projects. They believed that they had time on their hands, not anticipating the fallout of Enron, Bernie Madoff, Y2K, the housing bubble, the dot com era, or any future natural disasters to be so financially devastating within the first ten years of the new millennium.

Baby boomers once had a secure pension but they changed the laws to take advantage of that surplus. With the economy in recession and 78 million baby boomers getting ready to retire at the rate of 10,000 per day, there is not enough money in social security, Medicare, or Medicaid to cover all of those boomer expenses.

With regard to their retirement income, if you just multiply 10,000 boomers being paid from their 401k and/or pension per day each month - well you get the drift. It's probably more money than the national debt per year being paid out when you factor in the real numbers. And don't forget that there are no new jobs being created to support all of those payouts. Unemployment is and will continue to be at an all-time high. While you are still calculating, don't forget that many retirees will not see that matching contribution in their 401K as promised.

On a side note: *how scared and terrified would you be if you read one day, in a newspaper or book like mine, how corporate America really viewed your hard earn pension as being "a debt, a liability, or even grounds for filing for bankruptcy"? Well that is the exact sentiment that Fran Hawthorne states in her book, Pension Dumping. She traces the phenomenon back to the 1980s.*

If you really care to know what your sense of worth is to a company today, you must read who Hawthorne quoted in saying - "You're paying pensions to retirees, who have nothing to do with the ongoing operations. It's unfortunate, but retirees don't contribute any benefit to the company...." (Pension Dumping - page 17).

Sadly to say, last time I checked, it took those same employees to run it so that it can be operational today. Unfortunately, veteran bankruptcy attorneys like Harvey R. Miller who made that statement does not see the ethical and moral conflict in a statement like that.

So what about you who is still working for them? Well, just by that scenario alone, the stock market will begin to crash. As retirees pull money out of their retirement accounts at such an alarming rate, the market will begin its slow decline to a greater depression than has ever been seen before.

I say this because about two thirds of the market is tied to baby boomer's portfolio accounts that have been invested. Many of Generation Xers have yet to fully invest into their retirement plan or have a solid job to worry about saving any money right now. Not to mention that many companies are really not matching your 401K contribution even though they may say they are doing so. That's a lie within itself. So there is only one result as every boomer starts retiring at a rate of 10,000 per day. You, the employee, working at your governmentally secure job, have one very serious problem. You cannot pull your money out because you have one stipulation for being in maximum security. That stipulation, if you can recall when you signed it twenty or so years ago, states that the only way you can walk away with all the retirement perks of your secure job is if you retire, leave your place of employment, or die. And because of the choices that you have made to stay and play life safe, the only thing you will be doing is watching your hard earn money decline in your unsecure retirement account. The same one that you cannot even touch.

To make matters worse, for those who are already collecting their retirement, the government has already stated that it will not be matching your social security checks with the rate of inflation[xviii] in 2009. With the economy the way it is, they can easily do it again. Something else to consider if you are getting a retirement check each month or each week; the government can stop matching the inflation rate again. Better yet, they can also reduce the amount you were receiving in the first place at any time. And you cannot do anything about it because they are the law and they make the law to benefit themselves. And if you care to fight the government, it is an uphill battle that you will most likely lose.

When it comes to governmental issued contracts and funding, it can be gone as fast as you got it too. Every time you hear the government is broke[xix], you hear about the program cuts, grant funding cut backs, and government funded job cuts. The overall philosophy of the government is like the saying in Florida: "If Mickey Mouse is happy so is Florida otherwise expect a famine."

Doing the Rat Race

Every morning, my wife and I watch the news before heading in to work like most of us do. One thing that bothers me each day is hearing about yet another car accident on the highway. It is another person slaving away to provide for their family day in and day out at the risk of getting injured or killed on the "freeway"- so  much for being free. Maybe that saying was reserved for the afterlife party.

This is one of the reasons why I do not sweat a job. I will never drive more than thirty minutes to work if I have to drive in, else it better be T or bus accessible. I refuse to waste an hour of my time or more dealing with traffic, road rage, or accidents. The odds are, at some point, I will be the one my family is hearing about on the 6AM traffic news. No thanks; I will pass on the fancy house in the suburbs so I can waste hours each day to get to work on time. Is it really worth it is the question? If you are one of those people, have you ever asked yourself if there was a better way? And if you have, this is a good reason why you should consider network marketing.

One of the reasons I like network marketing is that it allows you the time and freedom to work at home when you get your business to where you want it to be. You will not have to do that rat race or mouse trap thing anymore. I guarantee you that some of us woke up on 9/11 and asked ourselves: Is this really worth it? Why am I killing myself over a job? Some of us have changed careers since then and others walked away with a new purpose or meaning to their life when they faced death dead on. Will you wait for that day to come or will you start now? I can also make this guarantee, one is better than the other and a whole lot easier to start part-time.

According to a CNN broadcast that aired mid-July, 2010, 14.6 million people were unemployed and 46% of them had been out of work for more than six months. I bet you not too many people would think that they would be out of a job for more than two years. So what exactly is America supposed to do with all these dependent people seeking some form of benefits from their government? Are we supposed to leave them in the streets to die out?

While Congress battled with the issue of continuing on with another unemployment extension for these people, our government was about to find itself in another crisis or Catch-22. What about those hundreds of college students who were graduating with no job prospects? Do you offer them benefits as well or do they run back home to mommy and daddy for the time being?

It was clear that these graduates had not worked long enough for their state to pay out unemployment benefits to them. So what do you do?

How long do you continue to fund an open ended unemployment pool? The answer is 1.5 years and then you are on your own unless you have children or disabled elderly parent living with you; that is the only way you will get some form of assistance from the government.

The media kept that story quiet and our government did nothing for them nor did they address these issues in the end. One of the problems with America today is that we are not living in the real world at all. Our systems are collapsing but our government keeps on lying to the American public, telling us we are in a recovery.

How do you embrace change when you are being told by the media that the economy is on track for a full recovery? This has been the message of the top leaders across the country for some time.

I continue to dig deeper in my research, I find the facts are contrary to popular beliefs, too. If anything, when you take into account all the other hazards heading our way, it is extremely hopeless and depressing. This coming depression will be the biggest ever seen because too many of our past mistakes are coming due.

In the end, both the government and corporate America will start denying benefits and turning away people. For the time being, our government is too blind to see that this is not one of those recessions that is going to go away. In the coming years, more layoffs will come and more people will die from starvation, malnutrition, or as a result of civil unrest[xx]. And what about the baby boomers still working right now?

The Scarcity Mentality

For those who have spent the majority of your life working for the same company, it might seem unlikely but you could well find yourself one day being escorted out of the office by security. First and for most, if security is there to walk you off the premises, it will be so that you do not make a scene or get violent. Second, it will be about theatrics; that walk of shame[xxi]. You will be walked out of the office like a criminal. You just never see it coming because you have always thought of yourself as an asset, at least in your mind, to the company you devoted your life to helping grow. Finally, you will notice that you are being escorted out like a slave ready to be lynched by the cruelty of the world you have hidden away from for so long. It's off to the unknown world of the unemployment line. The same one you have been able to avoid throughout those years and have no idea what it has been like except for the stories you have heard but you shrug it off as if it will never happen to you because you have a degree and you have experience. But here it is, unexpected.

Now back in the office, your colleagues are shocked and some feel bad for you. Others cannot wait to share the latest gossip with their friends outside of your department. The youngsters who have replaced you are indifferent to your departure. Of course, they too are blindsided due to their newfound job; unable to appreciate the foreshadowing of their own eventual walk of shame twenty years later will soon be coming like the vague memory of the previous cubical they now sit in.

But for now, a new page has turned for these youngsters as they move up the corporate ladder, securing their jobs by making sure they are the only one who can do it. Time will show that all they have done is make themselves the only line of failure. In my years of working a job, I have seen people try to make themselves the go to guy or gal. It always ends up back firing on them.

It is what I call the scarcity mentality, though. When we become so scared of being obsolete in our jobs, we find ourselves doing this often enough. Instead of gaining multiple skills, we do the reverse and start using titles that makes us the expert. Personally, I don't ever want to become the expert so that I force everyone to come to me and give me a boost about being the man with the knowledge. The 21st century does not have room for that kind of thinking really.

Today, in fact, you want to be as diverse as possible, learning multiple skills for the future rather than specializing with any exclusivity.

It amazes me when I see folks doing that at their job. You can easily see them holding back from sharing information as if it is some kind of trade secret. They will train you but not tell you everything that you need to know to be an effective employee. Sure, corporate America fed employees that philosophy since the late 1980s, after the first pink slips were given out and jobs began shipping overseas. People began to wise up about job security. For the past thirty years, you have seen this culture slowly making its way to the workforce and people have started watching their backs. Trust was thrown out the window a while ago and suddenly people were back stabbing you just to get ahead.

It is no fault of their own when you hear stories like that of the Hyatt Hotel Corp[xxii]. On September, 2009, when the media got a hold of this story, it seems as though the CEO decided to fire 100 housekeepers after having trained their replacement for lower-wage workers from a Georgia staffing firm. After they were trained, 138 of the established employees from three Boston area Hyatt hotels were let go. Governor Deval Patrick got involved and boycotted the hotel chain. They had done the same thing previously by replacing 98 housekeepers in August of that year with $8 an hour employees from a temporary staffing agency. Sadly enough many of these former workers were loyal employees for twenty years, making just about $15 an hour.

Luckily for those housekeepers, they got national attention that brought support that made a difference. But these outrages are common practices that normally do not get the attention they deserve. As recession lingers on, job cuts are now routine to the point that the popularity of temp agencies have risen all across America. Many provide the much needed expertise of corporate America. In laymen terms that means, contract workers, temp to hire, no benefits, no vacation time, part time workers, young and sometimes inexperience workers, and those who are desperate for a job that they will take what they can get for less. This is the new normal when it comes to downsizing a company. You are simply cheap labor for now. There are no guarantees or promises. If you don't work, you do not get paid time off. And big businesses are loving it because they do not have to pay out those liabilities and the same goes for those agencies unless you pay for those benefits yourself.

We all know that our reality becomes part of pop culture when Hollywood comes on knocking and decides to make a satire, in 2005, with Jim Carrey called *Fun with Dick & Jane* base on the Enron scandal of 2001. The comedy was a great success but I was not laughing. *Fun with Dick & Jane* was actually a remake of the 1977 version that brought to our attention a more realistic view of what life was really like at the turn of the century. For those who actually went through that ordeal, it was far from a laughing matter. If anything, it was a preview of the making of a realty show. Nonetheless, Jim Carrey's character did a wonderful job in masking the truth by poking fun of Enron a year after the debacle. The story line revolved around a factious company called Globodyne, which saw every employee lose their retirement and benefits due to the fact that all of the employees were heavily invested in the company's stock. In other words, all of their eggs were in one basket.

This was one of the funniest movies ever depicting how corporate America operated during the worse financial meltdown of the century. The scene that stands out the most in relations to this chapter was the one in which Jim Carrey was fighting his former colleague to get this job interview. Unbeknown to them, the line was 100 people deep, all waiting for their chance to apply for this one position that was available. In the line, you saw the same things. Both men and women lined up in their blue power suit, brief case in hand, ready to seal the deal. Have you ever notice how we all look like human androids – we dress alike, talk alike, and we are all fighting to fill just one open position. In a nutshell that is how corporate America operates-we fight our way into enslavement and shake hands with our master with a smile.

How long will it take?

I must ask you, how far and how long will you allow the injustice in your family to continue? Do you even have a dollar amount in your head that makes it worth the humiliation, struggle, or poverty that runs in your family tree? Have you even put into your mind that your family has already paid the price for that admission generations ago? Therefore will it be one more generation or two? When will you stand up for your dignity or is the job all that you have? Is that all that defines you when people ask, where is John at? And their answer is he is working late again. He has to stay late. Why did I not see Jane at church this past Sunday? Well she had to finish up some paperwork at the office. Jane is late picking up her child again. Is your life a depiction of the saying, the early bird catches the worm? Do you think your job really cares that much about you? When you leave, retire, or die while still working at the job, life will still go on without you. Your name will still not be on that plaque or signage, even after you have spent years working within that corporate building.

Look at how many generations of employees that are still living paycheck to paycheck in your own family. When are you going to stop taking it by the chin? Stop saying it is okay because I have to provide for my family? Generations after generations of your family members have done it. They are still stuck in the same boat. Some have just moved out a little further than you and I. The façade makes them believe that they have accomplished something. In reality, it is really small. Your children's children are still fending for themselves, struggling to get by. Jobs are becoming scarcer with each passing month, each passing year.

Once again, at what point do you start to compromise the very being of who you are as a person? If all Americans would band together for a common purpose and say enough is enough, then half the problems we have today in the job market would not exist. We would not have to deal with corporate greed, corruption, and injustice.

When you begin to compromise with certain things, accepting certain things that go on at your job, it slowly gets easier, each time that you do it. It's like telling that little white lie to our children; the type of lying we tell them not to undertake. Yet we accept these white lies as adults as if they were partial truths. If you never stood for anything in your life time, then your children will stand for nothing in theirs. You will make them pay the heavy price for never speaking up against inequality. We all must become aware of our actions, choices, and decisions in regards to how the future of our children will be affected by the choices we make today. Someone or something will hold you accountable for all of it in the end, good or bad. If to no one else, you will one day be made accountable to God.

Case and point, December 2009, starts off with the tabloids all over Tiger Woods for his alleged affair. Now, as a squeaky clean, good ole boy, the very image Tiger has portrayed to the American public as a super star golfer, he has raked in millions in endorsements. With all he was doing behind the scenes Tiger was living a double life. With all that he had achieved in his career, he went out and destroyed his reputation when he cheated on his wife. It was bad enough that he was cheating at all, of course, but it turned out that he had slept with over twelve women during his marriage. Unfortunately just like Tiger Woods and the choices we are confronted with at our jobs, the downward cycle begins that first time we make an excuse for ourselves and say it is okay.

To give you another perspective of what I am talking about, I will share a letter that was circulating among my colleagues at one of my networking marketing companies through an email blast. I have kept it with me over the years because the letter rings true in all aspect. The letter that you are about to read was written some time ago, in 2002.

A FREE MAN AMONG SLAVES

In the United States of America lies a large industrial city, site of one of the largest slave-labor camps. Near this center are community settlements where slaves live!

Each morning the people move herd-style from these slave quarters into the industrial camp. Each one is at his or her station at 9:00 AM. Here they report to their masters for the day's duties, and here, at these stations, they remain chained until the time of servitude is over – usually at 5:00 PM.

They have no choice as to how many hours they must labor. Sometimes they are required to work overtime until the master tells them they may leave. Each year they are told when to take vacations, for how long and when they must return. They have little choice as to how much money they can make, and they are allowed very little time for lunch or coffee breaks during laboring hours.

They remain in their chains in great fear because the master can punish them with the lay-off whip. It is said that even some slaves who are good and faithful have felt this whip. Day by day, year by year, they toil – until the master decides it is time for them to stop work. He then releases them to retirement camps where they are forced to sit idle and wait for death. It is well known that the old slaves who try to work are sometimes whipped with the 'stop the pension' whip!

I know these slave camps exist for I am a Free Man who lives among them. I am in business for myself, I am truly free. I arise in the morning at the time called for by my schedule for the day. I decide my own hours. I can even cut my lawn during slave laboring hours. I can vacation when, where, and however long I may please. I am free to take my coffee break or lunch time at my own choosing, and of course I can decide my own paycheck. Because I am not a slave I can choose to work where I please, I am free to stay in the city as long as I please or I may leave and do business elsewhere.

I have seen slaves sadly pack their belongings, forced to leave their city in search of a new master when their master decided to beat them down with the 'LAY-OFF' whip! Children sad because of changing schools, wives reluctant to leave friends and relatives, but because they are slaves, they have to serve where their master will let them.

There is a ray of hope! Every slave is entitled to buy his or her freedom. The cost is not too high - yet, it seems high to those that never have the courage to pay the price; ONE MUST BE WILLING TO BECOME HIS OWN MASTER! HAVE YOU?

Good Luck and Good Recruiting!

Cleve & Dulcie Pickens
Senior Regional Vice Presidents of Central Florida
Prepaid Legal Services, Inc.

I am in business for myself, I am truly free!

Those who have never had a job, you need to understand that a job plays a perfect role in a person's life. For the most part, you might not have thought about some of the things that I have written about a job or seen your job through the eyes of a slave master. But what's most important for those who have one is to understand why you must be disgusted at being at your job. That way you can push yourself and use your job as your motivator for why you need to become an entrepreneur.

Living the American Dream

Do you recall at the beginning of this chapter that I said your home is a liability? Well one of the main problems that people were having with the housing market comes down to the reality that no one could afford their house any more. American greed had hit an all-time high that now affects all aspects of our lives. Greed had spilled over from as high as the White House to even the smallest mom and pop business.

Getting the white picket fence house is one of the oldest American Dreams that too many of us have held on to at the turn of the century. During the tech bubble of the 1990s, too many people relied solely on their one income stream to support their purchase of their so called dream home. And when it was all said and done, a growing number of borrowers with otherwise good credit were heading into foreclosure[xxiii] after losing their jobs. Many people bought into the hype of a greed infested stock market and believed that they were all going to be rich. And it all fell apart because employees had relied on their jobs as their primary means for financing their first home buyer's purchase, without ever considering the possibility of a layoff. But over the years, prior to the housing bubble, we did get financially savvy, thinking that we can make money in the real estate market by simply flipping houses, doing fixer - uppers, buy and hold then sell, etc. All of those were great financial schemes that we created to produce another income stream by reinventing an old industry. But it did not work. The American Dream was filled with amateurs who were far from becoming expert in the real estate business. What they did see was an opportunity to get rich and professionals saw suckers who did not know how to read legal documents and understand investment terminologies such as CDOs, ROIs, and Subprime Mortgage.

It was not that long ago that people use to purchase their dream home and actually remained in them for thirty years or more. Before the housing projects or the creation of the suburbs, people were just grateful for having a place to sleep. The parents of the baby boomer inherited what we call today government subsidies and military funding that provided homes for veterans at dirt cheap prices, as a thank you note for their service. People in the 1960s and 1970s did not see the greed factors that this new generation of real estate investors saw. People were content to just purchase a first home and call it home. The idea of buying a house so you can flip it or do cosmetic work to it so you can sell it in a hot growing market was really a new concept that had gone way over board. Looking back at the subprime mortgage problems of 2009, you can almost say that

America used their home as an ATM machine to withdraw quick cash. Whether it was for refinancing, investment property, a quick sale, or a flip, it was all done with the greed factor in mind.

A greed infested market, though, the real estate market has caused the cost of a home to go up

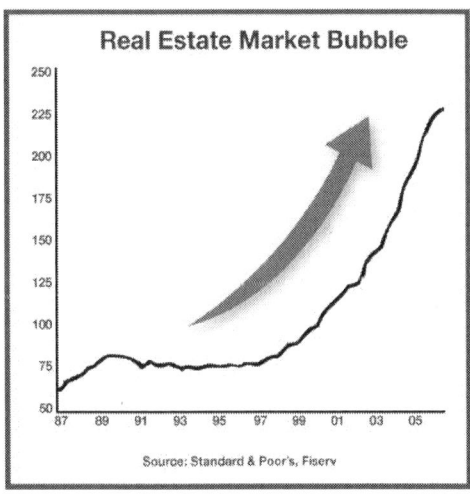

drastically. To some, it was not a problem. To those who were wiser and had foresight to know better, it was something that they did, in fact, see it coming. Those who had lived in their home for over thirty years saw green all of a sudden. The emotional attachment to their first home dissipated in favor of lots of cash or even a bigger place to live.

What we all failed to realize over the years that would lead to the housing bubble is that our paychecks do not increase at the same rate as the housing market climbs. Your average home ran as high as one million dollars. That was when I started looking at this housing boom as a joke. Who in their right mind can afford over a million dollars for a house? Folks may think their paychecks are increasing because of their three percent raise each year but they are not really seeing that it only reflects the rise of inflation over the years. So in essence, you are really making the same amount of money you did five to ten years prior. The big problem even to this day is that while you are enjoying that increase, taxes and deflation are sucking out the value left and right.

A great example that I can recall when I worked for the City of Springfield was that employees spent months fighting their unions to get them the raise they wanted. After months of discussions and compromises, they got their raise. Now, the irony of this story was that while we cheered for each other and patted ourselves on the back for a job well done, the systems that be had already planned how they were going to get that money back. And indeed they did. Soon after the city employees got their raises, guess who took it back by higher prices? The largest parking lot service provider in Springfield at the time.

I later found out that they were also well known in NY. Since Springfield employees mainly rely on their services to park their vehicles when they get downtown, that company found it fitting to suddenly raise the price of parking in the lots. The city employees therefore did not really get their raise. They just got an inflation adjustment for the coming year's taxes and cost of living expenses that they would have to cough up each and every day they worked. Meanwhile everyone was still hard at work thinking they were going to make ends meet with a few extra dollars in your check.

The following poem was sent to me via email, making light of how much Americans pay in taxes but don't realize it. It is truly a sad state of mind when you look at the truth; and especially the reality that so few have taken a stand to be financially free from a J.O.B.

Tax My What???

Tax his land,
Tax his bed,
Tax the table
At which he's fed.

Tax his tractor,
Tax his mule,
Teach him taxes
Are the rule.

Tax his cow,
Tax his goat,
Tax his pants,
Tax his coat.

Tax his ties,
Tax his shirt,
Tax his work,
Tax his dirt.

Tax his tobacco,
Tax his drink,
Tax him if he
Tries to think.

Tax his cigars,
Tax his beers,
If he cries, then
Tax his tears.

Tax his car,
Tax his gas,
Find other ways
To tax his ass

Tax all he has
Then let him know
That you won't be done
Till he has no dough.

When he screams and hollers,
Then tax him some more,
Tax him till
He's good and sore.

Then tax his coffin,
Tax his grave,
Tax the sod in
Which he's laid.

Put these words
upon his tomb,
"Taxes drove me to my doom..."

When he's gone,
Do not relax,
Its time to apply
The inheritance tax.

Accounts Receivable Tax
Building Permit Tax
CDL license Tax
Cigarette Tax

Corporate Income Tax
Dog License Tax
Excise Taxes
Federal Income Tax
Federal Unemployment Tax (FUTA)
Fishing License Tax
Food License Tax
Fuel Permit Tax
Gasoline Tax (42 cents per gallon)
Gross Receipts Tax
Hunting License Tax
Inheritance Tax
Inventory Tax
IRS Interest Charges IRS Penalties (tax on top of tax)
Liquor Tax
Luxury Taxes
Marriage License Tax
Medicare Tax
Personal Property Tax Property Tax
Real Estate Tax Road Usage Tax Recreational Vehicle Tax
Service Charge Tax
Social Security Tax
Sales Tax
School Tax
State Income Tax
State Unemployment Tax (SUTA)
Telephone Federal Excise Tax
Telephone Federal Universal Service Fee Tax
Telephone Federal, State and Local Surcharge Taxes
Telephone Minimum Usage Surcharge Tax
Telephone Recurring and Non-recurring Charges Tax
Telephone State and Local Tax
Telephone Usage Charge Tax
Utility Taxes

Vehicle License Registration Tax
Vehicle Sales Tax
Watercraft Registration Tax
Well Permit Tax
Workers Compensation Tax

STILL THINK THIS IS FUNNY?
Not one of these taxes existed 100 years ago,
and our nation was the most prosperous in the world.
We had absolutely no national debt, had the largest
middle class in the world, and Mom stayed home to
raise the kids.

What the hell happened? Can you spell "politicians?"

And.... I still have to "press 1"
for English.

Author unknown

So throughout that thirty plus years for those who are fortunate to still be at a job that long, you have raised a family and sent your kids to college on one pay check. While you are proud that you have accomplished so much with so little, you neglected to see all the other liabilities you have purchased while maintaining that one job or one income stream.

In hindsight what you have done is really show your kids how to be caught up in the same traps as you. Simply because you have been conditioned to assume that is the only way you can make it in America. By holding on to a job for dear life when the going gets tough and running to a second job, part time to survive if all else fails, is an endless cycle. Never seeing how trap you have become to one income stream.

And by one income stream, I do assume the household is consisting of both partners / spouses whether it may be in a marriage, domestic partners, or splitting the rent. All in all, your kids grew up following in the same footsteps. It is a cycle of oppression and the makings of a selfish generation that cannot be seen through the eyes of an employee minded person. Those who are high achievers or a high income earner will never see this as a problem because they can always work over time. Better yet, they can get another degree to please their employer and increase their salary or increase their skills to be more attractive to another employer willing to pay them more in the job market. Once again these same people never look down the road of life and ask themselves, how long can this charade last and how many more degrees can they get before reaching the glass ceiling or worst off, finding that they have made themselves over qualified for that same job?

By the time you realize what you have done to yourself, you are already obsolete. By now, your employer would have thanked you and sent you off to retirement with a nice going away party and given you that stupid key to nowhere, if they even still do that anymore. That golden key is really the irony of it all. Maybe it represents that asset you have been to the company for so many years. Well, your assets have really become obsolete because for most folks, they never picked up any other skills while being at their job for so long. They just bought into the belief system that you can work all your life here and get a nice retirement package. While that may be true for some who retired twenty years ago, it is really a lie for those who are just about to retire now. The second phase of your life has really begun. I do mean that literally. Those who have no other supplemental income have to figure out the 40 - 40 - 40 plan for the first time. That is to say you have worked forty years at forty hours a week to retire on forty percent of your total income.

TRADING TIME FOR A $1.00 BILL

Does your life feel like the image above? All you do is work hard for your money but it has yet to materialize to anything worth waking up for in the morning. Statistically, it is likely that someone entering the job market now will hold seven to eight different jobs before the age of thirty; they will have between 15 to 20 jobs over the course of their working life. Did you know that 97% of Americans spends their whole life exchanging time for a dollar bill but have nothing to show for it at the end of the year while the other 3% of Americans are leveraging their time to make their dollar work harder for them so they can enjoy financial freedom? Has anyone taken the time to teach you the concept of money? Has anyone ever told you that you should, "Work harder on yourself than you do on your job?" That "profits are better than wages (which is fine.) Wages will make you a living, but profits will make you a fortune[xxiv] (which is super fine.)"

The answer undoubtedly is no because you have never heard or participated in any form of personal development. All you have been taught in life is to trade time for money. That process is called linear income. Well, you probably know that when you stop working, you stop getting paid. Salaries, wages, and contract jobs are all types of linear income. Passive income, on the other hand, is money that you earn for having put in the time and effort on the front end while reaping the reward of your investment on the backend. You no longer have to work for it. The money keeps coming in. Most passive incomes require that you invest your time or money in the beginning. Some forms of passive income comes by way of a business, stock ownership, MLM, or property owner of some kind.

We were all taught to go to school, get some good grades, and find a safe-secure job with benefits. Yes those were the good old days when that concept worked. Jobs were secure and plentiful. And there was even a time in America where you could have gotten fired in the morning and by lunch time you were already working at your new job down the street from your old job. But we are talking about present day, 2013 where you can easily find a boss on your back every day telling you when you can go to the bathroom, take lunch, take vacation; telling you how long you can visit a sick family member, or mourn the death of a loved one.

Okay maybe that is not the life that you live. You have a better quality of life because you either came from money or you are highly educated and have propel yourself to a luxurious six figure income and live in a million dollar house. You drive the finest cars money can buy and you are living the American Dream. Although that maybe true sometimes those who make a six figure salary can be fooled to think that they are financially set because of their material wealth.

But how you spend your money after getting it is really what determines whether you are financially secure. Beware that as long as you are receiving a paycheck from somebody else, you are not in control of your financial future. Even those who make that much pay a price today. There is a higher expectation from you now than ever before that is based on performance, meeting quotas, and increasing the company's profits every quarter. At times, it may not even be feasible but they don't care. They are simply paying you for results! And no results mean no bonus for you or worst, that you're out of a job.

One bad quarter or a single stock market plunge can also leave you back at square one, looking for another job that pays equal to or higher than your previous employer. Some of you may even go as far as looking for a second job part-time just to keep up with your life style. Perhaps you try to work overtime. The stay at home wife may even offer to go back to work. However working a second job is still not the answer. The IRS taxes you more so you cannot really feel the difference. The extra change may feel good in your pocket but who are you taking time away from? Your children, your spouse, and family are being deprived of your presence. Is it really worth it? As time keeps on ticking, your children are growing up without their father or mother around to teach them about morals and values. Instead the television or the baby sister is doing it for you. Has your family become more of a memory at your office desk, your car's visor, or as your cellphone's wallpaper rather than spending time with them? Is coming home late at night to kiss them good night while they are sleeping all that you can do? I am letting you know that there is a better way!

The solution to your financial problems relates to how you view money. Whatever amount that you make, let's call it X, does not matter whether you are financially well off or a struggling middle class person. What we fail to understand when we get a job is that we are not given that money up front. You have to earn it. It is only a projection of what you could be making at the end of the year. We never account for the various pre-tax or post deductions that comes out of our check each week as it is poetically stated in "Tax My What." This is where we have to accept the reality that these deductions will never go away. If anything, they will only increase as the economy gets worse, leaving you with two choices: network marketing or entrepreneurship. I will make the case for both in part two.

For now I want to play a quick game that will test your financial literacy skills. I know we all think we are highly educated and smart about money but how well do you understand the words leverage and residual income? Because that good education followed by our safe-secure job with benefits never taught us a thing or two in school about investing our money wisely. A matter of fact, I bet most of us were never taught anything about finances, from elementary school to college. The majority of us simply learn about money from what our parents knew or we figured it out on our own from the school of hard knocks.

I want you to look at the next image and answer the following question: If you were asked to pick one of these two options which one would you pick, a penny doubling each day for thirty days or a million dollars right now? Now I don't want you to over analyze it. Just pick your choice base on what you believe is the correct answer. Don't cheat! The answer is at the end of this sub-chapter.

Question?

Would you rather receive $1 Million today or a penny doubling for the next 30 days?

Drive Time University

For those who are reading this book and wondering whether or not entrepreneurship is for you, I will say this. Do you really believe spending two hours or more stuck in traffic every day is ever going to change your current circumstances? You sacrifice so much of time preparing to go to work and traveling back home that you really do not put any time into thinking how much of your life is wasted just being stuck in traffic or just waiting for your public transportation to come. So let's do the math.

Let's say the average worker takes an hour to get to work and an hour to get back home multiplied by five days and multiplied that by fifty-two weeks in a year. What you get is five hundred and twenty (520) hours of wasted time being stuck in traffic and surrounded by road rage. Now I said that was the average American worker today. That is really not true. Due to our current economic situation today, you will find that most folks are working two jobs, live further away from their jobs, and are actually stuck longer in traffic more than ever before due to delays and unexpected car accidents just to make ends meet.

Have you ever paid attention to rush hour? It used to be 5 o'clock but now it's more like 2PM to 3PM, 5PM and 7PM at least is what I see in Boston. What about New York, Georgia, Florida, or California? Can you imagine if that was the same case for those other big cities in your home state? So 520 hours does not look as bad as 720 or possibly 936 hours of wasted time per year but it does matter.

All that time equates to a lot of unproductive activity. So if you were asked to convert that wasted time into days, you would get between 21 and 39 days. Now, within 24 hours of living, we must feed our bodies. What's feeding your brain cells?

Imagine what 39 days of not feeding your brain with knowledge or wisdom would look like? But we do it every day because we do not think of the compounding effects this has to our potential growth.

What if you worked on your own personal development during those dead times? That would equate roughly about 1.5 books per month or 18 books per year that you would have read. When you say you are too busy to read a book or we are talking about trading time for a dollar bill, what price would you put on your life sitting in traffic each day? Because whatever the value amount is, I guarantee you it is priceless. This is time you cannot regain. Those that do personal development are far apart from the rest of the world who are still trying to figure IT out. And had you done some sort of personal growth over the course of your life, you would not hesitate in answering the question about the value of a compounding penny per day.

People like myself who are in network marketing or in business for themselves, we utilize every minute of the day wisely when we find ourselves stuck on a train, bus, or a vehicle doing nothing. That is why we call that gap of time our "drive time university." It means that we are simply taking that down time to read a personal development book, read an eBook, listen to some training material, or listen to an audio book.

These are all positive things that are helping us grow intellectually and support our spiritual development as well. Is listening to the radio or quietly sitting there going to improve your life? Of course it is not. Then imagine how far you could get in life or what you could do with those 800 hours of your life waiting around.

Let's not even think about the time we waste sitting there at the airport because we missed our flight, the flight gets delayed, or canceled due to bad weather. What about those holidays? You gotta love traveling during the holiday seasons.

The point of me stating the obvious is simply to say, what an improvement it would be in the quality of our lives if we all increased our IQ by a few percent each year.

Where would you be financially if you took the time to understand some key concepts about wealth and personal growth? That is really what separates an entrepreneur or business owner from someone with an employee mindset. And once your mind has been expanded, it is hard to go back.

Could you imagine what the world would be like if we were all readers? Well at least reading the right books and applying them of course. We have all heard the saying, "knowledge is power" but we tend to forget another key fact in that statement. It is really applying that knowledge that makes it powerful. It's *The Slight Edge* philosophy that Jeff Olson talks about. It's not give me the power then I will do the thing. It's do the thing and then I will give you the power.

I know a lot of smart people who are readers but where are they in their life? Just stuck like most of us because they are not applying what they have learned to their own reality, their own circumstances. Either that or they are missing the "HOW TOs" in applying them. Unfortunately the majority of us are not readers. There is not a conscious awareness to expand our mind to achieve a greater purpose. That could explain why most people are like machines trading time in for a $1.00 bill. We think that we are too busy trying to make that $1.00 bill to desire a more *Purpose-Driven Life*. I am telling you that it can be achieved.

I want to close out with two stories that are one in the same. It's about the life of two hard working people that I got to know over the course of my journey to entrepreneurship. One of them was a colleague of mine a few short years ago. She goes by Doc. The other was a stranger that I befriended in Malden, Massachusetts. His name is Chin.

Doc's one wish in life is to see the sunrise from her bedroom. You see, she lives way out in Fitchburg, MA where she owns a beautiful house and a horse that she enjoys taking care of. Her commute is four hours a day back and forth to Boston each week. She, like most of us who desire the peace and quiet life away from the city, must wake up very early so she can get to work on time. She is out of her house by 5AM every day to catch her commuter rail. She wants to see the sunrise and sunset from the inside of her house instead of on a commuter train. She said her property is a beautiful site to see in the morning. In thirty years, she has hardly taken a day off. She is always working or trying to make ends meet to survive. And all she wants is a day to herself to enjoy the sunrise during the week without worrying about a thing.

Chin is an older Asian American male in his fifties, living out in Malden, MA, but driving about three hours each way to get to the Cape. He has done this commute in the same minivan for twenty years, working as an engineer. He has a wife and kids in college to support. He told me that he was not a stranger to traffic. He sees it both when he enters Boston and when he gets to his job in Cape Cod every day. His only concern is that he can make it to retirement before getting the axe. He still has a family to support.

It is estimated that over a life time, the average person spends 100,000 hours working. Now that number may even be higher when you see kids as old as 16 years old already working in the fast food industry as a vehicle for financially supporting themselves with no plans to further their education at times. Furthermore the average male changes jobs every 4.5 years and women every 3 years. Again, that number will be a lot higher for a younger generation of kids working today because they are no longer working for some extra change. They are already working at a young age to keep up with the rat race that they themselves have become trapped into. What's on their minds is all about making their own money and walking away from their parents rule as soon as they turn 18 years of age. And you can easily see the difference in the next image when all they do is work hard for money vs. leverage income.

Watch what happens to this penny over thirty days!

Day 1	$.01	Day 16	$327.68
Day 2	$.02	Day 17	$655.36
Day 3	$.04	Day 18	$1,310.72
Day 4	$.08	Day 19	$2,621.44
Day 5	$.16	Day 20	$5,242.88
Day 6	$.32	Day 21	$10,485.76
Day 7	$.64	Day 22	$20,971.52
Day 8	$1.28	Day 23	$41, 943.04
Day 9	$2.56	Day 24	$83,886.08
Day 10	$5.12	Day 25	$167,772.16
Day 11	$10.24	Day 26	$335,544.32
Day 12	$20.48	Day 27	$671,088.64
Day 13	$40.96	Day 28	$1,342,177.28
Day 14	$81.92	Day 29	$2,684,354.56
Day 15	$163.84	Day 30	$5,368,709.12

If you picked the quick million dollars, it tells me that no one ever taught you the law of compounding interest. The answer to your problem is very simple. Stop chasing after money and learn to make money chase after you. Meaning you make so much of it that you could not spend it all in your life time. Unfortunately most people are too busy chasing the wrong things in life to understand the difference. What's worse about trading time for a $1.00 bill is that the system wants us to buy into this new concept called *The Four Hour Work Week*. Now the question is on which side of that four hour work week will you be in? The one who has the leverage or the one being leveraged by a boss? Interestingly enough "10,000 workers per year drop dead at their desks as a result of 60 to 70 hour work weeks in Japan[xxv]."

THE PSYCHOLOGY OF UNEMPLOYMENT

You know something, I may not be a psychologist but I have considered myself a philosopher for many years. And both goes hand in hand when trying to explain the emotional withdrawal you go through once you have been through a layoff. It is not an easy task to have worked all your life and have your job strip from underneath you. Whether or not you are in your thirties, forties, or fifties, we all share the same anger inside having to start over again; depending on where you are in life, the ordeal can be just outright devastating and depressing. Since 2000, I have been privy to the unemployment line because of the roll coaster that is the IT field since Y2K. It has never been the same since. Thirteen years have already passed and I have been through at least four layoffs thus far.

I remember those days very well. I was just starting to settle down in my career. I was starting to make what I thought was very good money at the time, a few years after college. Suddenly here I was a few years out of college and student loans looming. Suddenly I found myself out of work.

Bills were piling up fast and I went through my savings real fast. I was on my own for the first time outside of the safety net of my college dormitory, enjoying life, and I was struck with a burden of debt. So I did what everyone else has done. I lived off my 401K for a time, until I could find my next job. A few years would pass again and I found myself in the same spot again. Maybe you were like me and took odd jobs, tried changing careers, or went back to what you know best because that was where you made the most amount of money.

You figured you had too many years in that field to start over again in a new field for what seems to be minimum wage to you. Well, I have been where you are right now. So much so that I thought it was important to give you some guidance as you go through these phases of unemployment.

By my third layoff, I understood the process and I took it with stride. I had already made up my mind that a J.O.B was not for me, the idea of becoming an entrepreneur was solidified as the only way to go. It became clear to me what was happening in the job market. I was being phased out because I saw too much, knew too much, was outspoken, and I would not back down. I was a threat to the system.

Here are the twelve things you need to watch out for when you get laid off. Keep in mind that these steps apply to first timers and not those who have been laid off two or more times. By then, you're probably a pro anyway and you know how to survive on less than 100% of your income. But most importantly you would have known how to play the game and take advantage of the situation to change your circumstances for good. Nonetheless I am going to prepare you for that emotional process you are going to go through because I have been in that hole before and I have found my way out each time around.

1. Anger and disbelief sets in

Like I have said before, depending on how old you are, you either will brush it off quickly and start looking for another job or you will be very angry at where you are in your life, having to be laid off. Some of you will still have kids to feed, high school tuition to consider, and most likely, how are you going to pay for your kid's college fund now. Others will be frightened about their retirement.

What is going to happen to your long term goals and dreams? And that is when you start to break down in tears. Having to look at your life from an older person's perspective and wondering how are you going to survive in this job market when no one wants to hire a gray-haired old woman or a balding man in their fifties is not an easy thing.

2.   Giving it the old college try

Some of you will quickly try to reenter the job market with no luck. You will call upon your friends who work at various companies, begging for a favor or maybe that hook up that you use to get. What you will find is that everyone will be holding on for dear life of the little that they have at their job. There are not too many opportunities going around to give your best friend a break. To each their own! Their jobs are on the line too. It's just a matter of time before they find themselves on the same boat looking for work too. To add to your disappointment, you are now finding out that there's a limitation of how long you can collect unemployment for base on your state's statistical percentage and the federal government's willingness to provide aide.

3.   Going through denial

By now, a few weeks may have gone bye. You have gotten your last check and you are now living off your severance package. You start feeling ashamed of yourself for not being able to find a job as quickly as you thought you would. You have the right degrees, credentials, even the latest certifications. Still no one wants to hire you. You still don't want to admit to yourself that you must start collecting unemployment to pay your bills. So you hesitate to call the hotline because your pride is in the way. Your view of those who are on welfare or unemployable is starting to change. You start asking yourself if this is how it really is. Finally, when you do call in, the system finds ways to deny you what you have already paid into. It's another hurdle you have to overcome. Life is very unfair right about now.

4.   Learning to live off less than you make

You now have done one of the hardest things about collecting unemployment, accepting that this is where you are at this stage of your life. So now you begin to figure out how to live off 50% of your income or less depending on what you used to make. Some of you will quickly cut back on your lifestyle while others will struggle to let go of some of the luxuries that you were so accustomed to having all the time.

You are starting to learn something about yourself, though. "I did not realize how much I spent on frivolous things." For the first time, you start understanding what your money was being spent on. Before it really did not matter because you had plenty of income coming in. You hardly paid that much attention to it.

5.   Show me the money?

Well, three or more months have passed and you have sent out hundreds[xxvi] of resumes. You even redid your resume several times. A few of you serious workaholics might have sought out a professional career coach in hopes to give you some pointers. While you may have a souped-up resume, this does not account for any real world experience applicable to the job market today.

Age discrimination, level of education, years of experience, or credit worthiness are all factors that determine your eligibility to get hired. However, these coaches are lucky that they still have a job themselves, since everything is done online. You are just a number on an application these days. No one wants to see you first, that's the last option after looking through your qualifications. Then it comes down to how much are you willing to settle for that job. So you keep on searching until you find that company you think will pay you what you are worth. Ironically enough, during the dot com era, everyone was employable since jobs were a dime a dozen. After Y2K and the stock market crashed, all of a sudden human resources had a whole list of prerequisites - criminal background checks, credit checks, Facebook, and other social network chatter checks.

6.   Leave me with some dignity

Right now you are finding that more companies are looking to low ball you into a much lower salary than what you were accustomed to. You are now at your wits end. You start to apply for all types of jobs out of sheer desperation but you are still hopeful to get back in your field of expertise because that is all that you know. It really is the only skill that you have mastered in twenty to forty years of working at the same job. However, jobs are no longer looking for expertise, they are looking at their bottom line only and that is profits. So a younger you for a lot less and fresh out of college with no experience is more attractive than a person with thousands of miles in an office environment is what they are really looking for. No one will tell you that, not even your highly paid career counselor or resume coach. Remember they too are just doing their jobs as well.

7.   Time to crack open that piggy bank

You have been keeping an eye on your bank account since your last day at work. All that you have saved up for a rainy day has been depleted. Borrowing money from friends and family is the last thing you really want to do and your ego is still fragile. Looking desperate in front of others is out of the question. After having contemplated the idea over and over again, you are ready to pull out your 401K.

Depending on whether you have kids or not, you may have done it sooner rather than later. A much needed vacation creeps onto the agenda as you look at that extra cash. You are finally relaxing a bit after all of these years. During the course of your working years, you skipped many vacations so you can work late, not miss any deadlines, or you just never had time for one.

8. The resume games

Six months have already passed by with no job prospects in sight. You are either over qualified or have little experience. Maybe you've been told that they are looking for someone with some recent experience; you have been out of the job market for more than a year. You are probably getting advertisements in your mailbox or via email about going back to school to get more of that same education that has not been working for you. Since they are looking for more qualifications, you're thinking shifts. Suddenly you are wondering whether you should go back to school to finish some course or other; perhaps even spiffy up you resume with a master's degree or two. Still, people who already have these qualifications are rarely better off. They are in the unemployment line right alongside you. Some of these same people are still paying for the first two degrees. Nevertheless that is the route many of us choose. If you never finished school or you are highly intelligent that becomes the overall assumptions to our problems in times like these. I will go into more details of our education system in the next chapter.

9.   Feeling like the world is caving in on you

Desperation and depression have become your two worst enemies. You doubt yourself. You feel like your sense of worth has been stripped away from you. Up till now you had always pride yourself on being an independent person; head strong. You were the one person people relied on when they needed help. People came to you not the other way around. A sense of freedom has been taken from you. Your job was all that you had lived for. If you are the breadwinner in your family, your manhood may even be questioned by your wife, girlfriend or others close to you. Suddenly you are seen as a dead beat by those who are still gainfully employed. Some of you will not be able to support yourself even if you had your unemployment check each week or had taken out your 401K. It is still not enough to live on. You might have to apply for some forms of government aide to survive.

10.   Reaching your breaking point

So here you are, barely able to keep the lights on or food on your table. You have been robbing Peter to pay Paul. Some of you have never even understood that saying until you had to live it yourself. Maybe you are playing the credit card game too-just paying the bare minimum so it won't get declined or paying off one credit card with another one. Maybe the heat or electricity has been cut off and your open door oven has become your most reliable heating system. Your extra blanket, sweater, or Snuggie is no longer enough to keep you warm at night. If you found a job, it is because you have accepted a lower salary just to pay some bills or keep a roof over your head for the time being. You took a lessor pay cut; either half of what you use to make or one third less from your previous income. You are at your breaking point and contemplating drastic actions. Worse of all, a few of you are contemplating suicide as an option now. We have all seen the news as a father kills his whole family because of where they are financially. It is a common action taken by Caucasian men or high income earners to escape their realty. If that is you, I hope you are listening to me and take that thought out of your mind. There are better solutions than taking your life and the life of those you love. Don't let a job defeat you. Don't allow your life to be defined by a job that was setup so that you will fail along your journey. Go seek some counseling from your pastor or speak to someone about it. Be honest and let others know that the idea is on your mind. They will help you get through it. If taking your life is not an option then the next big thing that is commonly found in low income families or amongst African Americans is to go to the extreme by robbing a bank or someone else for money.

11. Going through the roller coaster again

Many of you will be blindsided by a second or even a third round of layoffs as I was in my thirties. So step eleven is nothing new, it is an extra step. One that begs repeating with experience, if you find yourself getting laid off again. However there is one twist that you were not prepared for. It has everything to do with that lower paying job you took to survive. Unexpectedly, that lower paying job does determine how much you will get on your second round of unemployment benefits if it is less than one years apart. One thing for sure, you did not expect to go through this again. So now three fourths of your income has been wiped out when you did not expect it. This is when you will either change careers for good or, more likely, find a way to get back to what you were making per hour by consulting for a little while on your own. Perhaps you even go back to the same slaveship again because that is all that you know how to do. Business ownership or entrepreneurship is still the last thing on your mind but is a solution, a way out, and possibly the end of the cycle.

12. Starting over

There is definitely a 12th step but it is more tied to step #4, learning to live off less than you make. If you are a brave soul and you are not suicidal or tempted to rob someone or something then your alternative option is to file for bankruptcy. It can be a blessing in disguise if you learned anything from step number four. Keep in mind, your good credit is already jacked up. Therefore filing for bankruptcy is okay so long as you have learned from your mistakes. We, as Americans, have lived way above our means and part of our problem is doing exactly that, that we struggle to learn to live below them. Filing for bankruptcy only to return back to your old habits does not teach anyone anything about being smarter with our own money. The biggest misconception that you can learn from going through unemployment and bankruptcy is that we all thought we understood money. I am as smart as you are and I too thought I knew all there was to learn about money. However, being cheap, a saver, or conservative about spending your money does not mean you really knew anything about the preservation of money or wealth principles about money. Unfortunately all you did was play it safe and that is not the answer either.

BANKRUPTCY

"A sign of the times"

Let's talk about bankruptcy for a moment. It is such a sensitive topic that I almost did not want to bring it up. For most of us who have gone through some very tough times already, or are really struggling right up to the boomers' tipping point years, it is about to get ugly. As we all know, finances will get even tighter than before. As ashamed as I was once taught to believe about filing for bankruptcy, I no longer feel the same way anymore.

I understand from a business stand point, now, just how bankruptcy works. I understand the purpose behind it. It is a chance to get rid of all the bad habits or mistakes we have made in life when it comes to financial knowledge. I am not a CPA nor am I a tax expert. I am not here to tell you to file for bankruptcy but I am here to tell you that it is okay as an option. It is not the worst thing you can do in the world. You have been conditioned to think like that. However if you never learned the lessons needed to be gained from bankruptcy then you are doomed to repeat the same mistakes over and over again; even pass them on to your children and depending on how bad it gets, it can even spill over to their children for generations to come.

"Bankruptcy has simply gotten a lot cheaper, easier, and more socially acceptable than it used to be." That is what Fran Hawthorne had to say in reference to corporate chapter 11[xxvii] filing. And it seems particularly valid because consumer debt is at an all-time high today. Eventually people will have no choice but to file for bankruptcy protection. We have already seen this take place as they changed the bankruptcy laws on October 17, 2005. The government realized that too many people were filing for bankruptcy. To offset this problem, the systems changed the laws to make it harder for the average individual to be able to file for bankruptcy because Americans were way over their heads in debt. For the first time in history the consumer was doing the same thing that PBGC[xxviii] had allowed corporate America to do since the mid-70s.

Once again, history will repeat itself as the boomers' retiring will force the stock market, the housing market, and the rest of the U.S economy into a spiral that will eventually force at least half of the middleclass population to file for bankruptcy. They will simply be unprepared. Those that were mainly dependent on the government for a pension, savings, 401k, Social Security, and their family to bail them out will all find themselves in the same boat - in the unemployment line, the welfare line, and the bankruptcy line preparing to file.

However you want to put it, the majority of working Americans who will live through 2015 and 2025 will all share one thing in common. They all will have either filed for bankruptcy during that era or will have known someone who has gone through it. Going through bankruptcy will likely be as routine as going to the doctor for your yearly checkup. It really won't be as taboo as we once thought it was. And by 2025, if you have not filed by that year, it will become even harder to do so because the retirement of the baby boomers will have put a tremendous strain on the economy by then. Since the system makes the rules, they don't want you to be any wiser about getting rid of your debt. If everyone is doing it, then who else can they enslaved with higher interest rates? Hence if the economy gets into such a bad shape, no one will care if they have to file for bankruptcy. Again I am not here to give you advice on filing for bankruptcy but understand that those who do file prior to 2015 have a better chance of recovering from the seven years of bad credit ratings than those who try filing after 2015.

The reason why I say that is because that individual filing prior to 2015 will have smartened up about their debt and become a better investor. At least in theory, the hope is that one would be able to have more buying power to buy assets at a bargain than at a higher price later on when the economy recovers. However I don't expect this recovery will be as quick as we would like it to be.

CHAPTER 3
EDUCATION IS A B.S DEGREE

We have all heard the saying that hindsight is 20/20 but what does that really mean? Many of you may never have the chance that was given to me to see the world from two perspectives, one as a child growing up in the Boston private education system and the other as an adult participating in the Boston Public School education system both from the viewpoint of a teacher and an unbiased observer.

I saw life so differently as if I was living in two different planets going through the motions but in the same body. The experience alone has given me a new found respect for my mother, who raised me and my sister in a middle class family. I don't know how she did it but I am thankful that I was not raised the way I was in any other environment than the one God brought me into this world as. I am so grateful for having been raised as a Catholic, too, and for having had the opportunity of a Catholic education. Without it, my foundation would not have been the same. This book probably would never have been written.

The stories that I am going to share with you are not indicative of the schools that I went to or worked at but they are intended as a reality check of a broken education system; one that we rely on to educate our children with the little that we have to provide the best education possible. Later on in this chapter, I will share with you my journey as a child through my Catholic education. The differences are staggering.

Adolescent Eyes

In the mid-nineties I was still in high school, taking the bus and train to school like a typical student in Boston. At an early age, my point of view on education was being developed. I had a love for learning. My conservative values gave me an appreciation and a very high regard for learning. You can say that I was a nerd that developed into a straight A student. However, learning did not come easy for me and that was one of the reasons why I had such love for learning.

As my sophomore year progressed I began to have a lot of questions about the system that I was in. I was beginning to notice the inequalities of our school system as I would watch students my age commuting to school without a school bag or even a book in their hands. Occasionally I would see a notebook or nothing at all. I kept wondering what kind of education were these kids getting? How could they not have homework to do or school books to take home and read like I did? Aren't we all supposed to be the hope for the future? That was when I questioned the value of a private education versus a public[xxix] school education.

There was indeed a big gap in equality. I went as far as questioning the fairness of the system to even grade us on the same level on our SAT scores. Here I was taking a nationwide test and I felt like I was not being given a fair chance like the rest of those privileged kids that came from money. They had all the latest equipment that money could buy. We were still using textbooks that were decades old and torn up. They were already advanced in computers and I knew my school was far from having even a functioning computer in the classroom.

Was I being setup to fail already as a teenager, I asked myself? Yes, I may have gone to a descent school but I was not that far removed from those kids in the streets with no books in their hands or a school bag on their shoulder.

As I got older, I was watching my cousins preparing every weekend to take those entrance exams that would determine if they were going to get into the best grammar school or high school. Deep in my heart, I knew that it really did not matter. I recognized that your class and income level really was the thing that determined what your options would be at the end.

If you did not have the right scholarships or grants, if you did not know where to apply for them, all the best grades in school would not afford you the luxury of anywhere decent. It was true of high school and college for me and my family.

My cousins and I were first generation college students trying to climb the American education system for the first time with the help of our broken English-Creole speaking parents, who did not really know what they were doing. It was just an educated guess or the advice from a friend or colleague. At times many parents in my shoes would miss deadlines and were out of luck.

After college I stayed out there in Western Mass for three years before I had an opportunity to move back home and work for the very school system that I was raised in. I served as a substitute teacher and a staff member a few years apart. My first job back was working at Quincy Upper High School. It was an up and coming charter school that was transitioning from middle school to a high school at the time. It was very diverse, with the majority of students being of Asian descent.

In my year and a half there, I notice the drastic change between the 5th graders over the summer break and the 6th graders transitioning back to school in the fall, though. The best way to describe it was as a transformation of two different groups of students. The 5th graders were calm and respectful when they left for the summer. As 6th graders, though, they were a different breed of students; more rowdy, obnoxious, disrespectful, disruptive in class. Many had attitude problems and talked back to their teachers.

Myself and a colleague of mine were both baffled as to what took place when those same students went away for the summer and came back to school in the fall. We had the worse of the worse students summon their parent to the school and we did see where they picked up those habits. It was from their young mother who acted exactly in the same manner as their own child. Because the school was so diverse, we also saw a change in the behaviors of the same quiet, obedient and once discipline Asian students that we had come to love and otherwise thought we could count on. The bad kids had a greater impact on the kids you would not normally see acting up. One thing for sure, it did not matter what nationality or race these students were. Their behaviors were all the same.

My classroom experience was more about learning to institute discipline than actually teaching. For every new period that started, thirty minutes of it was wasted on quieting kids down, stopping fights, arguments, reprimanding kids for talking out of turn. And it dawned on me that these teachers were not trained to deal with the chaos that was Quincy Upper School in all of their years of being teachers.

At Madison Park High School, where I substituted for a day, things were not that different. The only difference was that the students were tougher, older, and more mature in the way that they acted out. Now being at Madison High School was not new to me. It was a well-known controversial school that allowed high school girls to bring their babies to a school-based daycare so that the mothers, could attend classes. It was the first of its kind at the time designed to stop an alarming rate of high school drop outs. Too many females were getting pregnant on a yearly basis that they had to put that system in place.

I remember one of the school days that I was there. The principal would walk around like he was a warden, making sure the prisoners were not skipping classes or hanging out in the hallways. The school had the atmosphere of a prison to me. Security was everywhere because of the school's history of fights breaking out.

These were my observations in 2002. Far from the type of education that I had received when I was a kid in grammar school and high school. Fast forward eleven years later, America has a new crisis in its hands that involves school shootings and a call for teachers to be carrying a handgun on them while in the classroom. It is a far cry for help from the days of Columbine to Sandy Hook Elementary School that has gotten the nation's attention. However school shootings have been going on in our black neighborhoods and schools since the 1980s and no one did anything to stop it.

It was not until it happened in the white schools with an AK-47 that it became a tragic epidemic for anyone else to care. But as you can see the other problems failing America's education system has been lingering on long before race mattered. School rage was already brewing throughout our schools regardless of race, gender, or sexual orientation. Our youth are not getting the proper education that they deserve. It is no longer a one race problem. It is now America's problem as schools all across the country have inadequate facilities, poor learning techniques, limited after school programs, and many other much needed services.

From inside the classrooms to the inner workings of the school system as a hotline worker for the Boston Public School's Transportation Department, I got to hear the voices of the parents who were merely teenagers themselves at times on the phone trying to find out where their child was. I would estimate many of these parents were between the ages of 20–40 years of age raising babies on their own. Struggling to make ends meet, work, and raise a child at the same time. The countless calls that came in were based on the life of a hard working single mom rushing to pick up their kids at the bus stop, kids being left on buses, kids being sent to after school programs on their own, kids changing schools in chaos, fighting on the bus, other people picking up kids at bus stops because parents were not around or too busy at work to come. Other calls involved problems with the inadequate bus operators who were always late arriving to the schools or the bus stops. Bus drivers were given routes that were impossible to follow. Issues over budget cuts and driver complaints about being over worked and under paid were also common but the list went on and on; how they made it work each school hear is a mystery but that was a public school education as I had experienced it as an adult.

Grammar School Education

My own American education started out with my parents having extraordinarily high hopes, as most do. We all start our children off wanting to be doctors and lawyers. But somehow those dreams fade away for most of our youths. In other households, there was no hopes and dreams, at times not even a purpose spoken on behalf of a child of God. There was no expectation of any success. That was more like my story. I had a childhood dream of becoming a priest one day but those hopes quickly seemed to fade; quicker than most, perhaps, because my family did not know that I had a learning disability while we were in Haiti. At first, I struggled through grammar school as an F student. Only when I got into a Catholic school in Mattapan, Massachusetts did everything change. Suddenly I became an A student and my earliest dreams looked that much more feasible.

In middle school, I was one of the top students in the class. I took advanced English and math classes. The dream of becoming a success story looked entirely reasonable. I was the pride and joy of my mother and teachers. I was a fast learner and was also maturing faster than the average student. I absorbed everything around me but I was still a slow reader. Everything did look easy for me. You could have also said that I knew what I wanted to be when I grew up. I always had high expectations of myself and where I wanted to be in twenty years when asked. But as all young kids grew up, plans changed with each new discovery.

High School Education

In high school, the idea of becoming a priest was at last a distant memory. I fell in love with science and technology. In high school I was certain that I was going to become an astronomer one day although those dreams faded as well by the time I got into college.

I was confronted for the first time with my learning disability. My decision to go to one of the best high schools in Boston, B.C. High, did not prepare me for a change of pace. It was one that I was not ready for since I cruised through grammar school never being challenged as I was to be at B.C. High. I struggled but still managed to hold on to a 3.0 GPA without officially being diagnosed. While most students my age were discovering girls and their hobbies, I was focused on my education and my relationship with God. I developed my identity through the help of the Jesuits who taught me throughout my four years. I still had hopes of becoming an astronomer but I was slowly developing a passion for technology and business.

During my years in school, we did not deal with the issues our children face today like school shootings, school fights, teenage pregnancies, kids committing suicide, and coming out of the closet, were things we heard in the news. The closest thing we ever experienced in high school was sports brawls and the occasional fist fight and that was it. In the end, I had selected B.C. High as my primary choice for high school because I knew it would shelter me from the public school system. Even to this day I am more proud of the Jesuit education that I received than my college education. My high education laid a solid foundation for becoming "A Man for Others." It is a principle that I live by ever since.

It is right about the time we started our senior year that the realities of the world came crashing home that all of our hopes and dreams may not come true after all. By now some of us would realize that we don't have the best grades to enter our college or university of choice. The gifts and talents that we had were beginning to wash away into fantasy land. A more realistic view of life and a career path is the conversation we've dreaded having with our parents. "Grow up and get a real job" are some of the words that rang forever in our heads yet no one taught us how to financially live as an adult. We were supposed to follow in our parents' footsteps or better yet our sibling(s).

College Education

After making my way through high school, I was in college all of a sudden, on my own to make decisions that would have a life time of repercussions that I could not imagine. Those who could not handle their new found freedom found themselves soon on academic probation. In college we are forced to start over again to make new friendships and a lasting impression. It is here we form new identities as well in order to fit in or remain the same while some of us are comfortable in our own skin. Many of us managed to fit in without missing a beat. Others adjusted and attempted to live with a total stranger with two very different personalities.

From being home sick our first two years of college to being settled in our dormitories swearing never to go back home by our senior year, we manage to make the best of a cramp room for two. Some of us learn to follow a syllabus and make life a little easier by staying ahead. We take courses that we like in hopes of meeting our core requirements and graduating on time. Meanwhile time is ticking and the real world waits for us to arrive, complete with our new found sense of responsibility and wisdom.

Those who had the pleasure of slacking off during their four years have to answer to someone now. It might be their parents, student loans, Fannie Mae, or Freddie Mac, but a financial promise must be repaid. Whether we understood our fiduciary responsibilities or not time was up and we now had to figure out if we all made the right choices in career paths and education to enter the real world with a job.

Many stayed behind to finish, some got side tracked, partied the four years they were there and flunked out of school. Others started a family early and were long forgotten during the course of school break. I saw many did what was a common excuse just to graduate. They found a major after several attempts at finding the right courses to take each semester so they can just graduate. Some of us did it in four years while others did it in five or more years; they could afford to pay for it on their own dime. Others just did not care and took every class under the sun until they found something with enough credits after four years to declare a major and get out.

The reality of college life for me was that it really did not matter what degree you got in the end as long as your parents who paid for it were happy that you had a piece of paper that claimed you were "educated" by whatever means you managed to get one. That is the reality today of a "good college education" for most students. Yet we hang our degrees up high on the walls of our office and claim we are educated because someone handed us a piece of paper saying so. In the end it was all a joke or was the joke on us?

Whichever way the wind blew seemed to be the direction of our sail after college. Some of us had hook ups waiting for us while others had to explain what they had accomplished in four years of a good college education. And to some it was all a daze and for others they were as confused as when they left high school. Those that could not figure life out on their own went back home to the same old thing. Only a few were left to pursue their life long dreams and career choices. If you were to ask many of the graduating classes coming out of college today, they still could not tell you what they wanted to be when they grew up. Sadly to say many have yet to accept that they were now the grown-ups.

I, in fact, was a workaholic and found my calling in the IT field while observing what was to be my college life experience. Like many who found their calling early, they continued on doing so in college and continued on with that same career path in the real world. Some of us got a different degree unrelated to our passion only to pursue a career in the field we hate. It is by far the most common misconception of adults. Many believe that we go to college to get a degree in our field of work and that rarely happens. In almost all cases, college students feel as though they only went to college because they were told that was the next big thing to do in life. They got a college degree for the hell of getting one at the expense of parents. Then they hardly use it in the field they study. And for those who actually do go into that same field often found themselves hating it once they realized that is what they will be doing for the rest of their life.

Unfortunately one thing that we were never taught in school by our parents or teachers was whether or not that degree matches the kind of income we wanted to make in the real world. On many occasions, people finish school disappointed with the degree they got because it really was just a good enough degree and they entered the real world with a bitter taste of resentment after seeing the tuition bill. That is when reality sets in. If we honestly asked ourselves the question, was it worth it, many would probably say no it was not, but we sure had a good time while it lasted?

All in all, it was not perfect but it was the best education that money could afford me at the time. But why was I special or any different from anyone else who wanted the same opportunities that I got? The difference was in the morals and values money afforded me. The privilege to have more of something as precious as choosing a college education versus going to an Ivy League school or a family tradition such as Harvard, Yale, or Princeton. My choice like many always came down to what I or my family could afford. And if it was not much, you got just that much education as well.

THE IRONY OF A COLLEGE EDUCATION

On my journey to college, I learned a lot of things on my own after entering the real world. And a lot of it had nothing to do with my college education but had more to do with having some common sense along the way.

More than fifteen years out of college, I have relied more on my business and common sense to get me through life than on what my college education taught me. Many of you who are in business can probably say the same.

If you are someone who is not a critical thinker and don't spend time reflecting on the things you have done in life then you just might miss a few ironies in life that I could not help realize myself once I was out of college and had begun pursuing my entrepreneurial freedom. Once you read these ironies you will see for yourself that our actions does some times borderline on the definition of insanity, if we continue doing the same things over and over again without expecting a different outcome.

- There is an interesting irony that we all learn once we are in business for ourselves. And it goes like this. The A student in school is so smart and always gets the good grades in school while the D & F students are always failing in school. So one day, after having been labeled a failure in school, the D & F student said he had enough and drops out of school. To survive, he started a successful business of his own. Years later, the A student finishes school and comes knocking on his door because she now needs a job. So that failing student gladly offers her a job in the company he created on his own because she was so smart to begin with.

- Isn't it amazing that as hard as you worked to get that good grade in school that no one has ever asked you for your GPA? If you think about it, no one has asked you for your GPA once you are out of school because in the end it really was all about networking. Yes, you do need an education but if you were playing the game right, you would be better off once you got out had you kept networking with as many friends as possible. Most students found it easier to network with others in the real world if they had participated in either a fraternity or sorority.

- Life after college can prove to be a Catch-22 since businesses want you to have experience before coming to work for them at the same time most graduates need that first job to gain that experience they are looking for. It just proves my previous point on networking and how important internships are.

- Does it not amaze you that most kids will spend 21 plus years getting an education but are never taught once how to manage their own money or anything about finance,[xxx] let alone how to balance a check book or how to live within their means. Some cultures do not even believe in having a bank account. And they go on to pass on that philosophy for generations.

- What a joke to have a degree but not be financially grounded. We keep teaching our kids to go buy into that old mindset when it is not even working for you. All you are doing is putting them deeper into debt than ever before. What is worse is that a degree alone cannot save your children from facing the worse economy they will have to grow up in because the very educated status quo of the political system that you believe in has been passing the buck on to the next generation since the Great Depression. So if nothing has changed, why do you think chasing a job is going to help your children in the 21st century? The current path of our education system no longer makes any sense. Parents, you need to start motivating even your children to become entrepreneurs of their own at an early age. It will be vital to their future.

- I rather be an uneducated fool who is smart about their financial future than an educated fool with degrees on the wall but financially broke or destitute and not able to see the writing on the wall. As my mentors use to say, "I would rather say I is a millionaire than I am a millionaire" with the money in my bank account to back it up versus a degree that shows that I can speak proper English but have no financial stability in an economy like this one, when my boss hands me a pink slip. Running to the unemployment line or standing in an interview line fighting for that one open position at a J.O.B with twenty or fifty plus candidates with the same degrees is not going to help in the short term to feed your family. After all has been said and done, that job is only temporary until your next pink slip or downsize.

- We send our kids to college only to live the rest of their lives living check to check. Let's not even add up the amount of student loans that had to be taken out for that education. What you have to look forward to is spending the rest of your life paying off that interest that continues to accumulate on top of that loan when in fact your life time earning potential does not equal to or above the amount you paid for that college education in those same four years. It does not make mathematical sense. And from a business perspective, that is not a good return on your investment (ROI.) The best suggestion that I can give you is to let them take the risk themselves instead of letting these loan vultures come knocking down your door or put a lien on your house or assets. Please consider the long term outcome then the immediate gratification that you helped paid for your child's education.

- Cosigning for your child's college education is not the smartest thing that you can do for them today. It is financial suicide due to their inability to find a job once they graduate. You are more likely to default on that loan than have your child graduate with a degree let alone on time to pay off that student loan. You are better off saving that money and invest in a business with them than to throw it into a college loan that cannot guarantee him or her a good job after they graduate. You are more likely to lose your house, get into more debt; and your child will still struggle financially chasing down job security for the next twenty years.

- To make matters worse, our children are getting themselves into a lot of trouble while in college. Within the last decade a large number of college students have found themselves coming back home as parents before ever starting their junior year. As you might expect, a young 21 year old male graduating college usually does not want anything to do with a new born baby and the responsibility of juggling a career at the same time. To his demise, he is instantly faced with child support for the next eighteen to twenty-one years plus student loan interest accumulating. What a way to start your financial future.

On the other hand you have students graduating from a big Ivy League school that had already cost an arm and a leg only to awaken to an unexpected financial mess as they enter the real world. Imagine, for example, your child going to Harvard or Boston College and they are studying to be a teacher. So I took the liberty of doing the calculations for a year's tuition at B.C. and tuition averages about $55,000 per year. So to waste $55K per year for four years and be paid on average of $35K-$45K to me does not make financial sense when there are cheaper colleges and universities that they could have attended to end up making the same amount of money for the rest of his or her career as a teacher. Mind you, this does not take into account the cost of living, transportation, food, and other basic living expenses. These are simply examples of how our children are being setup to fail without taking into consideration the reality of how much living on their own cost.

- The reality[xxxi] of a college education does not add up when students themselves don't pay attention to what they are doing to their financial future. One thing that is not discussed at the dinner table is that everyone expects to get their dream job after finishing college. With layoffs reaching about 15% in Massachusetts in 2010 and has already past that level in other states who is really in denial, the students or the economist? Currently in 2013 the national unemployment numbers have plateaued at 7.8% for the past three years. The reality of it all is that kids are finding themselves not even working in their field[xxxii] after college because they cannot find a suitable job to begin with. Another big disappointment is that parents don't realize that college students are spending not four years to finish their degrees but on average five or six years.

On the flip side, those who have a bachelor's typically run back to school to get a Master's degree so they can avoid student loan debts after six months because they got laid off or could not find work.

- There is a common misjudgment made on the part of employees who work full-time and go to school part-time in hopes of marketing themselves while climbing the corporate ladder. Many have experienced a rude awakening when they demand more money from their boss since they now have a Master's or PhD degree. The school of thought has always been that a Masters or PhD is what's preventing you from moving up in the company. What actually happens in almost all of these cases is that they are turning you down because your job expects you to accept the same pay for the job that you were currently doing. You've heard the routine excuses: you are already at the highest income bracket for your job description; there is no more money in the budget to give you a raise. To tell you the truth, the real reason is because your company does not see any need to give you a raise just because you now have another degree that you can hang on the wall. It has been my experience that the only way you will get to utilize the full benefit of that degree is to leave your place of employment and go somewhere else. The threat of leaving maybe the only thing that forces their hands if they indeed consider you to be a valuable employee. Otherwise, expect a change of employment or stay where you are. It is one of the most common assumptions that I see people make once they get their degree. Please note that even if your job tells you that is what you are missing from your resume, don't expect them to honor it a year later. It's usually a dare that they don't expect you to take on.

- This is my own opinion if you are serious about obtaining an additional degree or finishing the one you started. Do it for your own self-interest and not because you intend on moving up the corporate ladder or getting a better job out of it. There is no such thing anymore. Those days are over. If you cannot learn to fend for yourself, ensure your financial survival independent of your job, then you will always be at the mercy of your employer, your union, or the government to bail you out.

- Another mistake in thinking that I see folks make is that people sometimes never look at or care to find out how much would their job pay them after that raise. So what is my point? People will spend thousands of dollars on continuing education by taking out loans on top of loans with high interest rates just to be cap at a few thousand dollars at their job for the rest of their careers. At some point you cannot get any more degrees to increase your income. All you would have done is make yourself overqualified. In the end, all you would be is frustrated because you would have realized that you have spent a lot of years climbing the corporate ladder just to reach the glass ceiling. Meanwhile, that student loan is still coming in the mail with an interest that continues to accumulate because you are only paying the bare minimum payments.

Consequently there are others who really believe that another degree is going to resolve their financial woes. As if a another degree is going to solve their lack of money coming into their household. If they already have the bachelor's or Master's Degree, the most they may get is an additional $5,000 to $10,000 in pay while never looking at the cost of that raise. Regrettably, they will hardly ever see the extra income due to taxes and other deductions taken out of their pay checks.

I should point out that both Dr. Danko & Dr. Stanley[xxxiii] have done some extensive research showing the impact of higher learning. They stated that a higher education demands a higher lifestyle ideology. Meaning that the higher your education, the more upper class you become or desire to become. Before you know it, you start to fancy the finer things in life and you find yourself trying to keep up with the Joneses.

For those who have high degrees, I have to ask you what is it going to do for your children's future when they get older, aside from the income you make from it and provide for them? They cannot always get the same level of degrees as you. They may not have the same IQ you have to even get just one of those degrees. Not to mention the tremendous amount of influence and peer pressure they face from their age group. Most of you with high degrees have very demanding jobs. Sometimes the career path of choice takes you away from the home for long periods of time. So where is your influence and purpose being instilled in their lives? You are out traveling, attending business conferences, and lectures. In most cases, you do not have time freedom to spend with your family. So what good does it do having those extra degrees on the wall when your children are lost in the world?

- I personally find it amazing that college graduates seem to lack common sense the more education they have. It's as though the more education you pursue the more our systems have you dump the most practical ability to reason and have some street smarts. Somehow we seem to find a way to make everything more complicated.

- Have you ever thought about the process of elimination in regards to learning? It was one of those things that I managed to ponder upon once I entered the real world. If you think about it, we are sending our children to school so they can force us out of the work force. The students in exchange are replacing you the parents for cheap labor. You might not have looked at the process like that because we never think about our children directly forcing us out of the workforce. It is always someone else's kid that we see in the office looking to make that first impression. So why not imagine your child. Let's say they studied to be an electrical engineer. They are a chip off the old block and are as smart as you. They graduate with top honors and come to work for the same company as you. Eventually the company goes through cutbacks and they are laying you off while keeping on your child. Why? Simply because your child does not care about any benefits, stock options, pension, 401K, or vacation time built in. Well at least these are not their primary focus right now. They are still under twenty-five years of age and fresh out of college.

Nonetheless, all of those things are cost to a company's bottom line and it is a tremendous savings for them to let you, the parent, go right now.

But we never see that dramatic walk of shame where the parent is pointing fingers at their own child, saying, "you did this to me! All the sweat and tears I put in this company for twenty-one years and this is how you repay me!" Not that funny, right? If we really saw the world from that perspective, parents would definitely not sacrifice all that they have to get you the student that college education. It just does not make sense. But in essence, that is what we are doing every four years. Why is that? Again, jobs are moving overseas, jobs are being automated, and your child is entering the workforce earlier than ever before. In some cases, as early as 16 or 18 years of age and not going back to finish their degree. The bottom line is that there are not enough jobs being created. Everyone today seems to be looking more for a job instead of creating one themselves. It has become the hand me down effect on a digital generation.

Life after College

As it was customary of UMass Amherst graduates, most of us moved back to our home state to try and find a job. The UMass student population is largely made up of New Yorkers and Bostonians. Although New York and Massachusetts are two very big states, I was somewhat dumbfounded when I saw the same people I grew up with, went to school with, and now work in the same town as I do living average lives struggling to make ends meet like me. It made me feel like I had not achieved much to still be hanging around the same people I went to school with. Some of us will spend the rest of our lives in Boston and never travel outside of the state or visit another country. It is at these moments in time that I pause to ask myself whether or not it was worth the experience when I look at my life and my four years of student loans. Then reality sets in again when I find myself next to a cubicle with another individual who never stepped foot in college or followed the same traditional path that I did. Only a handful of us are actually doing what we wanted to do out of college. And even fewer than that are living above average lives. Upon reaching the epiphany of life after college do we realize that we were just a bunch of "worker bees" as Z would put it in Antz.

PICKING UP BAD HABITS

Has anyone told you about the habits that college students pick up in school that actually sets them up to fail for the rest of their lives? Many of them do not realize what is going on until after they enter the real world. It all starts off honestly, the day they step foot on a college campus. If you've been a student, you probably saw the big banner in front of your student union building telling you to come and learn about all of the school activities on campus. You got caught up with the fun activities setup to grab your attention and distract you while you were busy filling out those free T-shirts or gift cards in exchange for creating a new bank account or signing up for a new credit[xxxiv] card.

Fresh into college, you are taught to start building up credit and so you begin accumulating as many cards as possible. Before you know it, you have the points reward credit card, the gas card, the travel or the mileage cards. It gets even worse if you are a current student in college today because there are so many new tricks and traps that you have to watch out for like the Capital One and American Express cards with their sassy commercials to suck you in. Even companies like Dunkin Donuts are cashing in on it too. Do you recall Chapter 2 on the *Idiot Box*? Well, Dunkin Donuts have a great commercial that teaches our youth to get in the habit of swiping that credit card in line instead of paying cash for your items. What ends up happening is that our kids are taught to go to college and put their books on credit cards and even pay their lunch meals on credit cards.

And to make matters worse, new companies like Higher One are forming to capitalize on your child's ignorance about their student loans. Companies like these are turning over student loan payments as an easy access ATM card that your child swipes everywhere they go.

On a personal level, many college students are so logical and sophisticated that they cannot grasp the basic concept of love or how to build relationships in their personal lives. They sometimes enter into destructive relationships that leave them scarred for life. Many start smoking pot or doing other recreational drugs that usually leads to heavier drugs. Some of the more commonly learned behaviors includes binge drinking, partying all weekend long, and drunk driving.

On a philosophical level, some of our highly educated children can rationalize why God does not exist or is not needed in their life. It seems that science can explain God as well. These are the same folks who are baffled when they cannot use science to explain strange things that are beyond our physics or what others call miracles.

The Good Ole Days

Boy, how much do I miss those good ole days of indentured servants, when you learned a skill or trade and created a business of your own. If you think about the structure of our school system, it is really no different from chapter 2 on *Conditioning the State of Mind* because the habits we pick up early on in life, from kindergarten through college, do teach us habits that actually condition our state of mind. There are systems in place to condition the way we think or act and socialize with others. All of this is done to shuffle you through the system so you can have an employee mentality. We hype up degrees as if they were the best thing since slice bread. So we can all have something to chase after.

In the 1940s and1950s, when a high school degree was good enough, only a few people could afford to go to college. And college was really reserved for the elite class of society. It meant you came from money to have a college degree, most of the time. When our society started to change economically, the rules began to change too. By the 1980s, folks were able to move up and make stride in corporate America. So the system decided to raise the bar again by having these new educational requirements. A Master's or a PhD became the new standard to work towards since everyone could afford to get a bachelor's degree. It was the new way of distinguishing intelligence by having an MA, MS, or PhD after your name-all in all separating those who could financially afford to get one too. Today it is the standard for excellence and classism. It's just the system's way of separating the haves from the have not's

A few years ago, I attended a business conference and learned about Rodney and Thao Sommerville from Mooresville, North Carolina. They had achieved the highest level of success in network marketing by becoming millionaires in three short years. Although that was impressive enough to say the least, that was not what got my attention. The Sommervilles were two highly educated people in corporate America but were still financially struggling to make ends meet. They both worked more than 60 hours a week and had nothing to show for it. They were maxed-out with credit card bills, student loans, a mortgage, and a car payment. They were both overworked and underpaid looking for the American Dream even though between the two of them they actually had seven (7) PhDs. Yes I said seven. It is a true story that opened up my eyes. And it was not like they had low paying jobs. Rodney was a city engineer and Thao was a benefits and compensation analyst. Their story alone was shocking for me and it should make you rethink your plans.

I know it is easier said than done having lived in Boston, Massachusetts for more than twenty-five years, in a state that is known for having the best schools across the country. It is one of Boston's pride and joy. However I am not alone in my thinking. I can recall the day my pastor referenced his PhD in theology to the congregation. He said although he does not need it, he got one anyway for those who might question his intelligence or authority as a bishop. Since we are such an educational driven state, he did not want to leave any doubt that he could not get one for his wall too. And that is still a reflection of Bostonians to this day. In essence I said all that to let you know that it no longer matters any more. That too is part of the old ideas of the past. Bostonians may choose to hold on to that façade but let it be known that even people with PhDs are getting laid off too. They are also getting downsize as well. That piece of paper alone cannot pay the bills today nor will it in the second half of the 21st century because a different level of skill sets will be required for your survival.

In the 21st century, the nature of the game has changed. It is no longer about the color of your skin or nationality but rather about your financial status. How much do you have in the bank? What is your net worth? Don't get me wrong, if you have a few thousand dollars in the bank or even a little over six figures. That is good for you but what I am talking about is big money-a few million dollars in the bank. Cash on hand aside from other investment money; money that isn't tied up. That is how much the game has changed. We are in a time where greed is about to reach a tipping point and the system is trying to financially squeeze everyone out who cannot hold their weight in gold.

Don't forget that your definition of financial status is no longer determined by how much you make. It is really determined by not only how much you make but also how much Uncle Sam gets to take from you after all of your deductions. In other words how many things can you write off legally yourself as your CPA keeps up with all the new tax laws that are so ever changing? Today's tax laws favor the rich and wealthy vs. the poor and middle class. It is said that there are more words in the US tax code then there are in the Bible.

Let me say this about tied up investments: regardless of the potential gains from these investments, they are not actual gains until they become cash on hand. It is digital money you are playing with. The stock market proved me right, as did Madoff and the real estate market. Simply put anything can happen in a matter of seconds or days. Take a look at what happened during the dot com era. The job market had changed from seeking benefits to stock options. Now who really benefited in the end? Of course it's your job. The dot com generation did not care about health benefits. So there was no expense on the books to show for it. But on the other hand, millions of shares were divvied up to employees most likely at the highest cost per share to them.

The stock market, by 1999, was at its highest levels ever. No one expected it to come tumbling down. As we all know that's just what it did soon after in 2000 but definitely in 2001 after 9/11. And who had the most to lose? All of those employees who took the stock option deals. Now I don't mean to call anyone fools but they were. When the market was going down and companies were closing shop left and right, not too many people thought it was wise to sell their options. Instead, people bought into the hype from their broker, friends, or CNBC special expert analysts that came on the show every day and told you to buy more cause it looks even better at $20.00 than when it was at $50.00. And America also bought into it. We all did! Nevertheless all bad things that felt good must come to an end!

This was why after the fall out, CNBC changed their policy requiring full disclosure as far as any commentator's involvement with any stock they spoke of on the show. Prior to that, it was like insider trading at its core. Brokers, analysts, CEOs – all were telling folks one thing but were dumping their stocks on the back end.

On a side note: *here is a trick I learned at a seminar about what CEOs were doing after the Martha Stewart incident. They can easily avoid insider trading by swapping shares with another CEO's company. For example, I tell John A, from company XYZ to buy preferred shares of the exact amount into my company. In return I do the same for him in his company, WXY. So when things don't look too good for any one of them, they simply call each other up and say sell. And it is all done legally. There are no laws being broken. Hence creating one of the loopholes for continued insider trading. Once again the system at its best.*

REAL WORLD LESSONS

Every year from May to June, college graduates finish their last year of college and head out into the real world. Each dressed up appropriately with their notepad, binder, or briefcase ready to take on the world. What many have failed to realize is that timing is everything. For me personally, it could not have been any more perfect since I was entering the IT field in 1999. The market was booming for young technicians like me straight out of college looking for work. The opportunities were plentiful for anyone who had entered the tech bubble that year. However, it also made me realize a year later that the jobs that I was able to get in 1999 had nothing to do with my degree. In fact, my degree had nothing to do with me finding a job right out of college. It had everything to do with the timing of the economy. It was further proof why your degree did not really matter in the end. It did not matter what kind of degree you got. What really mattered was the economic climate in which you got out of school that determined how successful you would be right out of the gate. You could have had just a Bachelor's, a Master's, a PhD, or a GED. It did not matter because jobs were a dime a dozen. Anyone could find a job. Even dot comers were jumping from job to job within six months or less for more money someplace else. It was a free for all until it all crashed.

Afterwards, I watched a college friend graduate with similar background and he could not find a job. He had the right education, the right degree, but no one was willing to hire anyone. It was nothing more than another wake up call to me about my college education. Years later I would hear a business colleague of mine iterate these words at a business meeting. "Your degree is worthless by the time you get out of school." I was as shocked as you are right now. I did not want to believe it. He went on to explain and used a doctor as a good example. His point was that a doctor's degree, like any other graduating senior, was obsolete as soon as they walked out of school. There is always something new to be learned in the medical science field since technology keeps changing every day. By the time you get out of school, like a depreciating new car from the lot, the information that you had learned is already old. His overall message was in favor of continuing education and personal development.

In light of the previous chapters, one must realize that they cannot spend their whole life in school learning. At some point, you have to go out into the real world and put that knowledge to some use. Most importantly you have to pay back those student loans a.s.a.p. But what if you are like the class of 2009[xxxv] that Katie Couric interviewed on CBS? They were four recent college graduates a few years ago with all the hopes and dreams of finding a job. Instead they found themselves unemployable working entry level jobs as secretaries, in fast food restaurants like McDonalds or a Best Buy as it was the case for Jessica Piperis, a Stoney Brook University graduate. Others who could not find work found themselves back home at their parents' house hoping for a phone call back. Pooja Jaitly was one of the brave students who spoke her mind and said, "I think that … having a college degree is so common… I think it is like what a high school diploma use to be." When I watched that interview, it was live but on the replay and online, they cut off the rest of her sentence because America was not ready to hear what else she had to say about her college education.

The reality is that students don't watch the news and they don't follow the trends taking place in the real world. They are taught to believe that just because they now have a bachelor's degree they are guaranteed a job. It just does not work like that anymore. That was just the wise tales of the 20th century. In any case had they been taught anything about personal development in high school, they might have picked up Kiyosaki's book - *If you want to be Rich and Happy Don't go to School.*

It could have saved them at least from all of that financial mess by the time they got out of college. More importantly than that, had they been watching the State of the Union addresses by their current President at the time, they would have heard the message loud and clear as to what corporate America is looking for.

In recent years, since I started doing Voices4theVoiceless,^{xxxvi} I began to notice something that I myself was not privy too when I was in school. If every parent would get their children to watch the Presidential State of the Union address each time it came on, they would have given their children a clear sense of guidance before entering high school and college as to what they all should be preparing to study if they really wanted to get ahead in life instead of letting them go play video games or hanging out in the malls.

When I first understood what the State of the Union addresses were about, it opened my eyes to the future of job creation. Folks the State of the union address tells you what you really should be getting degrees in to get these new jobs that are being created. Remember what I have said before, your old jobs are not coming back. Everything if at all possible is going digital or paperless. I will speak more on the subject in part 2.

So what could have been done to avoid this educational bridge to nowhere? I am glad you asked! Here are some of the things I learned and observed about the real world that the education system will never teach or tell you. They have become my real world lessons in life had I had a chance to do it over again. These would be the choices that I would make and discuss with my children when it became their time for college. But no matter what your philosophy on education is today, you need to be honest with them and allow them to see the reality of today's education because your children are watching your financial choices regardless of your conversation with them at a young age.

The first honest conversation should be about their ambition, goals, and their purpose in life. Now, had you applied the first chapter into their lives, that process would have been a done deal and an easier one to move forward with. If you have not instilled any principles of hope and courage into them, then you have to make the hard decision to ask them the truth. You have to ask them if they think or know that they have the drive or ambition in them to do something big with their life or not? Because school is an investment whether you want to look at it like that or not and if we are here to talk about being smart with our money, we also must be realistic about making good investments with our children's education.

Now, every child is different and that is why it is always important to speak purpose into them at an early age. I also realize in saying that, boys generally mature later in life than girls do. But I do believe that every parent know their child best to know whether or not they are serious about their goals in life or the desire to start on a life plan for success by the time they turn eighteen.

College is one of the most critical points in our child's life and we should not waste their potential by not planning for this crucial step. It is sad that we spend more time planning for our vacation than we spend planning for our financial freedom. We know all the steps we have to take to get to that final destination spot but we do not have a clue when it comes to our financial lives. Planning these next steps with your children should not be that hard unless they do not really have a plan.

If it is the case that they do not have a plan then you need to make that tough call of letting them know that you will not waste your hard earned money to send them to one of the most expensive schools of their choice for a so-called "best education money can buy" experience on you. They can either pay it themselves or take out their own loans because you are not cosigning anything.

Better yet speak to them about option two. Option two is also a practical thing that they should do in case it does not work out for them in school. I say that because college dropout rates are at an all-time high for many reasons than what our parents' generation would classify as losers for not finishing school.

Today the dynamics that affects students range from stress, medical leave, lack of funding or aide from school, broke, teenage pregnancy, family obligations, a business opportunity, to who knows what can come unexpectedly.

So labeling someone a college dropout has many meanings and personal paths that are all complicated. For that reason, I suggest you tell your child to go to school and make sure that they go for an associate degree first before attempting to complete a full four year degree. With all the uncertainties of the economy and life getting in the way, you never know what will happen. So play it safe and be prepared to at least walk away with an associate degree then spending four years to find yourself in limbo and be labeled as a college dropout. I think it is a waste of money when you still have to pay back those student loans and still have nothing to show for it on your resume. That was the mistake that I made and I wish I had someone wiser to tell me about getting one first.

This leads me to the second conversation which is the third option that your child has in pursuing a college equivalent education. And this third option is by far the best one of all in my opinion. It is also the only option that saves you a tremendous amount of money. Simply because it requires you to have real world experience to know what you want to do with your life instead of going to school and try to figure it out after college. It is also the option that I wish I really knew about instead of the traditional path straight to a four year college that really did not do anything for me financially. What I am talking about is realizing that you or your child was not made to go to college or spend thousands of dollars not using their degree after college which is more common than ever before. What I am suggesting is that you get them or yourself a certification in what you love to do or feel is what you are good at. For example, I was always involved in the IT field since high school and knew most likely that I would pursue it as a career path. What I did not know at the time is that I could have easily gotten a Microsoft certification which is more important in the technology world than paying for a four year college education. Subsequently I have discovered that this is true not only of the IT field but of nurses, accountants, CPAs, real estate agents, stock brokers, web designers, executive secretaries, and many others. They really do not require a college education for those career paths. What they require is on the job training, real world experience, and finally a credited course certification that goes with it. But the education system wants you to believe that to get ahead in life you must have a bachelor's degree or more for any field. I disagree. If you really want to be successful in life and you really want to get ahead in life, you must become an entrepreneur of the 21st century.

Why must you go into debt between $40K - $125K every four years or more to say that our kids got a college education? Maybe you think that you have done your job as a parent. When in essence all you have done is put your child in the same eight hours a day jail cell that you call a cubicle and make pretend that you are really progressing in life with a 3% raise that is really a 3% rate of inflation adjusted each year just to blind you with the truth. Maybe you will wait until you have finally reached the epiphany of your life at retirement age to tell your children and grandchildren that you really could not afford to retire on 40% of what your full paycheck use to be or that they should take the time to consider self-employment when they get older because of your hindsight which is really insight to 40 years of slave labor. Maybe you will accept the truth or maybe you will not.

Nevertheless to not be bias, I must say that if none of the above career paths are not of interest to you then you need to get a college education. Especially if you are looking at becoming a lawyer, doctor, politician, scientist, astronaut, astronomer, physicist, a teacher, etc. Let's be real, I myself would not want you to operate on me if you did not have a medical degree to begin with. Therefore these are all higher educations that require you to have a Masters and/or a PhD. But beware that none of these career choices can free you financially[xxxvii] from a destiny of slave labor until you make the choice to become an entrepreneur. I can honestly say all that without reservation because I know *"The Purpose of an Education."*

THE PURPOSE OF AN EDUCATION

This is the missing piece to my college education. In 1996, I was a student at the University of Massachusetts Amherst with Marcus Camby[xxxviii]. He was an upper classman and I was a freshman at the time. He was cheerfully accepted by the world media and fans when he chose to leave school early in his junior year to be eligible for the NBA draft. No one cared whether or not he was going to be labeled a college drop out because he had a career lined up in the NBA making millions of dollars. I, on the other hand, leaving in 1999, would be deemed as a college drop out because I went off in the real world to pursue my dream of becoming an entrepreneur.

By society's standards, I was a failure because I had no talent or money to back my decision. I just had a burning desire to build my own company. I also stand a better chance of unlimited success through the duration of my life than Marcus Camby after his career in the NBA ends. I have a better understanding of money and business than Camby, with his claim to fame in the sports world. Having a lot of money thrown at you at a young age does not mean you know anything about money. It is a known fact that on average 60% of these players will go broke within five years after retiring[xxxix] from the NBA. The sports arena is a doggy dog world, with an average career length of about 4 to 12 years tops, if they can make it pass injuries.

His temporary success and exposure to lucrative contract deals does not necessarily make him any more educated than I am about money. If anything, Camby may end up like most sport stars who never plan

207

for life after the lime life is over and when the money runs out. They simply lack the proper education, legal, and financial guidance to make it in the real world long after their careers are over. Therefore his seventeen year success in the NBA will make him be like most sports stars that lived it up and have nothing but materialistic things to show for it. Many have no real assets or investments. They are just collecting a paycheck for their talent. There are only a handful of players who are smart with their money to invest it and start making their money work for them. I will explain this further in part 3 of *"Wealth Principles."*

Marcus Camby is no different from any other sport stars[xl], allowed to skip school to practice for a big game, cheat on their exams, or given passing grades to play. If anything they were the ones cheated out of an education. Suffice to say that this experience and others that I have observed over the years left me with a lot of unanswered questions as I pondered what was this so called education going to offer me.

For starters, why are there two sets of rules for achievers and average people when it comes to education? Here are the unspoken rules in today's society about education that is being told to average people. If you plan on being an under achiever in life, then go to school, get a safe secure job with benefits. If, on the other hand, you desire to be an overachiever, seeking fame, riches, the spot light, and Hollywood is in your forecast for the future then don't waste your time with a college education. You do not necessarily need to go to school is what the world seems to be saying because society does not measure achievers by their degrees but rather by their talent and ability to make money.

When I watch celebrities on TV, rarely do you find one with a college degree. I would estimate that a large portion of the entertainment industry only has a high school diploma or some college level education. It is probably a handful that has one degree, let alone a

PhD after their name. These hidden messages tell us that society will respect you for it if you are entertaining. Trust me on this one because our children and the boomer's grandchildren all have been paying attention. They see the mix messages that we as adults have been portraying to them on TV and in the media. They have been watching us carefully not by what we say to them but by what we do with our money. The reason behind this phenomenon is due to the reality TV era that we are in. Everyone wants to be famous, noticed, or be recognized because this new generation of teenagers only have money on their mind, living it up, and experiencing the high life of independence.

Unlike the rest of the world who follows the natural course of life's direction, (grammar school, high school, and then college) these disturbing questions left me wanting more than what was being offered to me through the education system. What I witnessed during my four years of college also said a lot about our education system. Mainly what is it really designed for? Is it really there to educate or rather put a certain class of people in line? Was it designed to mold our behavior and conform us to what limited expectation society has for us? Lastly is an education there to play into the minds of those average folks and make them believe that they have a sense of accomplishment by seeking a college degree or going for the crème de la crème, and obtaining a PhD? In the end, this thing we call an "edumacation" is mainly for those who just don't get it.

Over the years, I had more questions than answers that made sense to me. For some reason, the majority of folks did not see the bigger picture or conspiracy against the education system since they have been conditioned for generations to buy in to it without question. I on the other hand refused to accept the status quo. The older that I got midway through high school I detested the idea that someone was going to hand me a piece of paper. As if I was still an adolescent being told, here you go, take this diploma and put your head up high and call yourself educated. Now run along your merry way. The truth of the matter is I would be no more than an educated fool if I accepted the status quo and smile while being insulted by an education system that was filled with lies. Our education system today is nothing more than a hypocrisy and an insult to your intellect.

Have you ever questioned the status quo only to wonder why are some people able to have a better quality of life than you have? If you have not done so then that's because you think within the box instead of thinking outside of the box of life.

You may not have heard of Ivan Pavlov and his research but the systems in place have used his knowledge and expertise to control you indirectly. Ivan Pavlov is a 1904 Nobel Prize winner for his research on conditional reflexes that causes dogs to salivate when in the presence of food. In other words, his research is a form of controlling animal behavior. Better yet science has come to use his research to understand how humans can be conditioned to conform to a certain way of life. Thus the carrot that is put in front of us is that great paying job to follow once we get that degree while being hand fed for the rest of our lives.

If this information is not convincing enough, than you need to understand the reasoning behind the creation of the Rockefeller's General Education Board in 1903. That is how far back the conspiracy to control you and I have gone back. It was explained in G. Edward Griffin's book, *"The Creature from Jekyll Island"* in 1994 (pg. 555) and quoted by Robert Kiyosaki (pg. 32) in his book, *"Rich Dad's Conspiracy of the Rich"* in 2009.

Due to its importance, I will quote it again.

The Creature from Jekyll Island, by G. Edward Griffi:

" ... The purpose of the foundation was to use the power of money, not to raise the level of education in America, as was widely believed at the time, but to influence the direction of that education... The object was to use the classroom to teach attitudes that encourage people to be passive and submissive to their rulers. The goal was-and is-to create citizens who are educated enough for productive work under supervision but not enough to question authority or seek to rise above their class. True education was to be restricted to the sons and daughters of the elite. For the rest, it would be better to produce skilled workers with no particular aspirations other than to enjoy life."

The last sentence explains that as long everything in life is being provided to us and we are basically in a state of contentment or "rejoicing" and we will not have a need for anything else. Now for those who do not know who John D. Rockefeller, Sr. was, he was one of the richest men of his era. His name is synonymous with wealth and the high class of society. That is how important the name Rockefeller was and still is even to this day. So for him to be the founder of this General Education Board says it all.

It's no wonder our education system is nothing but a B.S Degree! If you go back after the civil rights movement everyone was ok with just having a high school education or none at all. Well that was true of the whites in a segregated America. All of a sudden things had to change quickly because colored folks were obtaining their liberty to be freed, educated, and vote. So what can the education system do but what would come naturally of course. Change the rules and make it tougher and add more requirements to get a job. After decades had pass, your education was no longer about separating the color line. It became a question of power. Who is controlling whom? Therefore everyone who was poor or middle class got lumped up together. Some of us still think the game is about white or black power.

Before closing out this chapter, I am going to share with you a factious story about slavery but the story has more to do with the way you define freedom and slavery vs. your philosophy on education. It is more on the line of *"A Free Man Among Slaves"* in chapter 2.

I want you to go back in time with me to the dirty South, just months before slavery was about to end and African Americans were about to be emancipated by President Lincoln. A few southerners were inclined to free their slaves long before Lincoln felt compelled to free any Africans on a national level. We all know that the north was mostly in favor of freeing slaves from captivity. Before there was ever a Harriet Tubman to create the Underground Railroad for slaves, slaves were escaping and heading towards the north. And that is where our story takes place.

Imagine you were a slave in the Deep South and all of a sudden, one day, your master tells you that he is going to set you free. He fills out the paperwork and hands it to you. Signed, sealed, delivered, you are now a free man amongst slaves. So you leave the only plantation that you knew of as home and headed north. Barefooted and penniless, you march proudly up north with your declaration of independence in hand hoping to start over where blacks were free to roam the land and considered an equal.

Along your journey, you ran into some slave catchers. They stop you and ask you what business do you have being on these roads? You tell them that you are heading north; that your master has set you free. The slave catchers look at each other with a smirk on their face and smile, really! They ask you for your papers to verify this. After confirming it, they look at each other again and laugh at your face. He goes on to rip the document up into pieces and then throws it in your face. One of the slave catchers then tells you to go about your business and be gone from here. Off they went on their horses, laughing and hollering about the incident and you remained dead silent as tears fell down your cheeks. The one important document that validated your existence was now gone, torn to pieces. You are at a loss for words.

Now I am about to ask you this very important question. If this man continues on his journey through the south and attempts to make his way up north and gets stopped again, what would you tell a white man who sees you wondering the field with a gun in his hands? He will ask the same question, what are you doing slave, trying to run away? Who's your master? How do you prove that you were freed by your master? Hence the most important question of all for you right now, is that man still a slave or a free man? Your answer should be a YES or NO, with a reason why you would make that choice. To tell you the truth, there is no right or wrong answer but only a reflection of how you see yourself by the degree that defines you on your office wall. My answer is in part 2.

TOP RANKING ENTREPRENEURIAL SCHOOLS IN AMERICA 2012

It is fitting since we are talking about becoming an entrepreneur that we take a look at the colleges and universities that do offer degrees in entrepreneurship. I should also point out that there is a big difference between taking classes from the School of Management (SOM) versus going to business school and entrepreneurial school. I must clarify the reason for doing this because it has been my experience after college that people are often confused, similar to me being in the IT field and having a computer science degree. The two are unrelated to each other but the real world does not distinguish between the two. For example, a computer science degree teaches me how to program in computer languages like Java, JavaScript, C++, PHP, Perl, Cobra, and HTML. These folks simply write codes that make the computers, Apps, and software you use function. I, on the other hand, am a field technician. My job is to fix the hardware or software when it malfunctions. Therefore I work with the physical aspect to a computer. I don't program anything.

Likewise, an S.O.M student tends to take business courses in school while a business major in college tends to study the management of a business or usually employees. These are your managers in corporate America. It can be tricky when you hear people tell you that they are going to school for business. What they are really telling you is that they are actually going to school to manage people; to be a boss in a corporate setting. If you are serious about doing business or starting your own business then you best find a university that offers courses or even a degree in entrepreneurship not a business degree. They are far from being the same thing and I hope as more people become entrepreneurs they will educate others on the differences.

Unfortunately for me, I did not know of any entrepreneurial schools that existed at the time. All I ever knew of was Harvard and I sure did not have Harvard money to be going there.

Today the education system has come a long way for entrepreneurs. There is even distance learning, which was just getting started when I was half way through college. Today the concept is called online learning or e-learning. One of the most famous schools that you can attend at the comfort of your home computer is The University of Phoenix[xli]. Today, every major college or university offers online classes. The University of Phoenix, however, was the pioneer of the industry.

On the next page, you will find three different references to entrepreneurial schools and some other business schools. I did that so you can pick which criteria you want to select for yourself or your child. In all of my research, there was only one school that stood out as being the best for business and entrepreneurship. I also did not want the facts to be bias since I am from Boston, Massachusetts but Babson College has come up at the top or near the top of the list of every search that I undertake for top entrepreneurial schools. It was always in the top three schools.

On average if you look at the tuition cost of these top ranking colleges versus what each student makes right out of college, on average, the salaries[xlii] are usually between $3K and $5K apart from the tuition, meaning it is a smart choice. They have dollar cost average for their income in the real world with a business degree to what the yearly cost is to go there.

In about five years, they would have been able to recoup their investment back in full. And that is the difference between being above average and paying top dollar to go to an expensive school, becoming an employee at will living paycheck to paycheck. These students eventually go to work for someone else to gain experience first then start their own business or just go right out of the gate and start their own companies. They don't have intentions of spending the rest of their lives working for someone else. They are taking charge of their education and starting their own business afterwards.

The Complete 2012 Business Schools Ranking[xliii]

1. University of Chicago
2. Harvard
3. Pennsylvania (Wharton)
4. Stanford
5. Northwestern (Kellogg)
6. Duke (Fuqua)
7. Cornell (Johnson)
8. Michigan (Ross)
9. MIT
10. Virginia (Darden)

2012 Entrepreneurship Schools Ranking[xliv]

1. Babson College
2. Stanford University
3. Harvard University
4. MIT
5. University of Pennsylvania - Wharton
6. University of California - Berkeley (Haas)
7. University of Texas – Austin (McCombs)
8. Indiana University – Bloomington - Kelley
9. University of Arizona - Eller

10. University of Southern California - Marshall

Below are the results of Entrepreneur Magazine and Princeton's review of the top graduate and undergraduate entrepreneurship programs.

Top 25 Graduate Programs for Entrepreneurship 2012[xlv]

1. Babson College
2. University of Michigan (Samuel Zell & Robert H. Lurie Institute)
3. Brigham Young University
4. Rice University
5. The University of Texas – Austin
6. Washington University - St. Louis
7. University of Chicago
8. University of Virginia
9. University of Arizona
10. University of Washington
11. University of South Florida
12. University of North Carolina - Chapel Hill
13. Temple University
14. Oklahoma State University
15. University of Utah
16. Cornell University
17. DePaul University
18. Acton MBA in Entrepreneurship
19. University of Missouri-Kansas City
20. University of Louisville
21. University of Southern California
22. Tulane University
23. Columbia University
24. University of Maryland
25. University of Oklahoma

Colleges and Business Schools
Top 25 Undergraduate Colleges[xlvi]

1. Babson College
2. Baylor University
3. University of Houston
4. University of Southern California
5. Washington University - St. Louis
6. Brigham Young University
7. University of Arizona
8. Temple University
9. University of North Carolina – Chapel Hill
10. University of Oklahoma
11. Syracuse University
12. University of Missouri - Kansas City
13. Northeastern University
14. University of Maryland
15. Clarkson University
16. Miami University
17. University of Utah
18. University of Dayton
19. Belmont University
20. DePaul University
21. Baruch College – The City University of NY
22. Oklahoma State University
23. Bradley University
24. Lehigh University
25. Texas Christian University

CHAPTER 4
ECONOMIC SEGREGATION
-THE RACIAL DIVIDE-

THE COLOR OF FREEDOM

Affirmative action was once a heated conversation amongst activists and protestors who believed African Americans and other minorities had not been given a fair chance to succeed. Somehow and somewhere towards the end of the 20th century, we stopped talking about it anymore or we hardly remembered what the cause was all about. Many white Americans believe that it has no relevance in the 21st century. Today more Caucasians probably think that they are the victims and that African Americans have had enough time for reparations. Regardless of what anyone thinks, the color of freedom today is no longer a question of white or black, who's wrong and who's right. There was even a time, black America was quick to say that "the man is keeping us down." There was also a time when the words racist, racism, prejudice, or discriminating were quick to come out of our mouths to classify the injustice being done to us. Today, it seems that these words are less often used to explain economic hardships. Everyone is in the same sinking ship, drowning in debt.

As much as we are worried about discrimination, racism, and prejudice the color of freedom is GREEN. I think too many of us today have gotten it twisted. It's about economic segregation not whites versus blacks anymore. The system no longer cares about that. The new game is about who is stacking the most money.

It no longer became an issue of how the system is going to continue slavery, persecuting minorities, and the less fortunate. Those in power began realizing that the middleclass was moving up. Minorities were allowed to have an education, move up to better housing, own businesses, access government grants, and take out business loans of their own. So the shift changed by the 1990s, as we all began to profit from the economic boom. Our society became more diverse. People lived in integrated neighborhoods, interracial marriages were common, and kids listened to all types of music regardless of color. Our mainstream life style became more acceptable and America truly became that Melting Pot that Dr. King, Jr. imagined it would be one day.

The system in place saw this as a profitable opportunity to change the game completely. Money was no longer an issue of race, color, or creed, since everyone had their own and can afford to buy it. The new war or fight if you want to call it that now became about economic empowerment.

Society has determined that everyone who works has a house, rents, or pay bills will become part of this new racial divide I call economic segregation. The system found and created new ways to oppress you and keep you from your hard earned money. If there is any way to penalize you in the form of fees, interest, taxes, miscellaneous charges, they will find a way to make you pay.

It does not matter if you have good credit or bad credit, whether you have been paying your bills on time or not, whether you are a good law abiding citizen or not. They will find a way to seduce you, entice you, and at times even use your children against you to buy them materialistic things of no value to your household.

Before long, you find yourself living paycheck to paycheck, pilling up credit card debt, and no longer credit worthy, even for obtaining a job. Oh, wait a minute that is old news. That has been going on for a long time now-so you say. Yes, that is true but have you notice the new add-ons? Your good credit is now attached to your job application, your car insurance, and your driving record. And you wonder why I call it economic segregation?

The color of freedom is GREEN! Folks it is no longer about your skin color. It is down to the color in your wallet, your purse, or your bank account. That is all that matters today to be financially free. And those who control it are making sure that you have as little access to it as possible. No matter if you are black or white; rich or poor. Yes, I did say rich, because rich is replacing and becoming equivalent to being middleclass and also because rich is only temporary. I will come back to this topic in part 3.

So what about you?

People do not realize that we are really fighting one battle, the haves and the have not's. In other words, this is where the rich, the middleclass, and the poor separate. You will either be rich or poor. (There is a third elite class. It is called the wealthy and I will come back to it in part 3.) There has been a driving force to get rid of you in the middleclass. The time is near. America has dumb down its citizens so that the middleclass can evaporate slowly but surely in the coming years. It is all so clear what our systems have allowed to take place with the next generation to come. The foundation on which this country was built on is slowly withering away-freedom, equality, and education.

The evidence is overwhelming when someone was stupid enough to make enough noise so America can try and support the concept of Ebonics in the mid-1990s. Who in their right mind would allow black Americans to start speaking in a broken tongue just because some of us are too lazy to pronounce our words correctly? Well the school boards of America approved it. And guess who followed suit, young impressionable Caucasians who want to be cool. Once again, America is fighting one war at home, not two.

Maybe for some of you the second war is the over population of the prison system. To demystify the false accusations, there really are more white men in prison than black men combined. So what about those of you who are returning to society? How do you survive in an economically segregated world? You really cannot! And it is designed that way so you can go back to jail. With the Rockefeller Laws in full effect in NY and some district attorneys trying to look good on paper in their next election, it is easy to find yourself facing trumped up charges. What most folks don't know is that the prison system is a big money maker. It is actually part of the economic enslavement that the other side of society lives in and no one cares to talk about.

Over ten years ago, I got a chance to sit down with Rev. Hutcherson,[xlvii] who has spent the majority of his career working with the men's prison ministry in Boston. It was him that taught me all about the prison system and how it is a big money maker. You would be surprised to know that you can build a city out of one prison system in the desert. Rev. Hutcherson went on to say that you can put a prison in the middle of nowhere and a city will eventually form around it. It will start off with the bare essentials like transportation to take families back and forth so they can see their incarcerated loved ones. After a while it becomes too much of a hassle to travel that far out. So a motel becomes a hotel, restaurants, fast food chains, gas station, laundry mate, employees, prison staff, homes are built, churches, schools, daycare, a police department, a playground; all this becomes necessary to accommodate visitors and a community is created right before your eyes that later becomes a town or a city.

It is a hard life for people like Dwayne M. Campbell and Mr. P[xlviii] who have gone to jail. They are two men whom I had the opportunity of becoming friends with during my years as a computer technician. Although society says once you have done your time, you are free to go about your life, well that is not always true.

The system makes it hard for people with a past record to obtain a job. Good men like Dwayne and Mr. P have spent their whole life trying to make ends meet. Sadly enough, Dwayne died on October 7,

2011, months after having been forced to quit his job because he lied on his job application in fear of a CORI check. He once told me that jobs overlook him each time he stated that he had been to jail. After the economy went bad, he got desperate and lied for the first time and was later on forced to quit for having a seventeen year record that should have been sealed or found to be irrelevant. Due to the stress of unemployment and bad health he kept an illness from his friends and family because he did not have any insurance.

Dwayne was a good, happy go lucky man who made some bad choices, like Mr. P, when he was young. He had, however, been paying for them up until his death[xlix]. Unlike Dwayne, Mr. P had an entrepreneurial spirit. I have spoken to Dwayne many times about going into business for himself but he refused even the thought of self-employment. Mr. P and I, on the other hand, have shared many found memories and stories about our journey through entrepreneurship. He has relied more on his business skills to survive then relying on a job offer. Mr. P, who is over fifty, has since graduated from college with a business degree from Cambridge College. He started an online store and has been involved in the network marketing industry with me. He has since married a lovely lady and enjoys growing his own fruits in sunny Florida. For the past ten plus years since I knew of Mr. P, he has created job opportunities for himself and as well as independent contractors in the past. Mr. P's life after prison is a good enough story why every reform prisoner must seek to be an entrepreneur rather than an employee. Simply because "the system is grossly unfair and you never know how much until you have to fight for your freedom."

So what about you, my hard working Caucasian friends? It may be shocking to know this coming from a Haitian American male who is not at the same economic status as you right now but I actually wrote this book more for (you) white Americans than African Americans/blacks, or minorities despite your contrary beliefs from the context of what you have read so far. I know that there are many of you who are rich or well to do that are thinking that these issues that I have brought up in the book do not affect you. But on the contrary every Caucasian or rich family in America should all be worried. I want to compare what has happened to you since the stock market and the real estate bubbles have crashed in the last few years.

During those crashes who do you think lost more, whites or blacks? Who has more assets, whites or blacks? Who has more to lose in the next few years economically, whites or blacks? You see black America has been fighting for a piece of the American pie for centuries and have not even come close to being equally yoked. Minorities have been fighting for their economic survival for more than four generations. It is nothing new for us. We are nothing but survivors. May I also add that there are millions more African Americans and other immigrants to this country who do not know what a stock option is, have a 401K, pension, bonds, annuities, have saved up six months to a year of income for emergencies, do not own a house or even have a vacation home to speak of, and don't have a savings account let alone a checking account in their name. It's a fact that white America and the rich have more to lose than anyone else who has stuck their neck in this economy or who has built a financial nest egg for themselves in the past twenty years working as an employee. You see the game has turned against you and you did not even know it.

You my friend are the economic group that I worry about. You who still have the white picket fence with the 2.5 kids; the two parent household; the kids in private schools or boarding schools still living that so called American Dream. You who have never felt the experience of losing your job, who wakes up when you are finishing sleeping, you who went through the worst financial crisis America had ever seen since the Great Depression but it was only a hiccup to you. You may have lost a few hundreds of thousands of dollars or even one million dollars but you are still moving on, you are still hanging in there. You may have already recovered in 2013. You my friend are the people that I worry about the most. Because you have yet to face adversity, you have yet to know what struggle means, or what it means "trying to make ends meet."

You may be a house wife or a stay at home mom. Regardless of your marital status, it is a statistical fact that you will outlive your spouse or significant other. Women are living longer, are more healthier, and live a more stress free life than their partner who are usually the breadwinner. Just as I stated about your life's cycle in chapter 1, women live happy ever after with the young stud enjoying your hard earned cash. On the contrary that is hardly the case anymore for those women who are left holding it down on their own. Many never bothered to learn about the maintenance of the household. "My husband or he always took care of that" is the common phrase that comes out of their mouth when he dies or leaves her. Some of these women will still have young children to take care of and send to college. Many of these women have been left in the dark about managing money or even know anything about continuing their man's business. I know that you may say to yourself, this is the 21st century not the 1950s but I can guarantee you that many women today are still living like that. And it is a hard thing starting over in a world dominated by men and the greed factor. In part 3, I will cover why it is so important to become financially literate over your money. You may think that it is a good thing that your husband or man left you with a lot of money and that you do not have to worry about anything for the rest of your life. Well I can promise you that is further from the truth if all you knew was how to spend his money. Having spent your whole life with an old fashion man who prefers his woman to stay home has been a disservice to you and a trap in itself long after he is gone. And vultures in suites will be watching and waiting for you.

Therefore I must ask you once again, so what about you? Do you think you can escape economic segregation too? Remember that the color of freedom is green, tangible assets, investments, and no liabilities like the ones I have referenced. Are you financially literate, business savvy, own your own businesses, and have multiple streams of income coming in to you or do you just have a great paying job that offers you the luxury of a six figure income? That my friend is the million dollar question.

COMING TO AMERICA
-THE LAND OF OPPORTUNITY-

There is an unspoken word or invincible baton that is passed on when foreigners come to America. I even feel it from my mom that she expects me to do better. It is an unspoken language that my generation of foreigners speak, believing our goal is to finish the race.

It is what's expected of me and every none American in the US. Statistics show that more foreigners become millionaires in this country than American born citizens. Why is that? Is it that unspoken message to become successful or is it poverty that makes us hungry for a better quality of life? I know it is one of the driving forces pushing me towards greatness. Successful entrepreneurs like Donald Trump, Robert Kiyosaki, and even Warren Buffet agree with such a statement. Nevertheless it seems as though Americans do not get it or do not understand how this can be, even though they were born and raised here. So what is the difference in our genetic makeup that drives us so much?

Maybe it's because American born children today are blind to the opportunities[1] that lay in front of them because they have so much that was given to them. There is no value in having so little today. Our children live in the here and now mentality— the gimme, gimme syndrome.

When we look at the sacrifices that our ancestors made to come to America, however, and consider the progress of our nation today, it is easy for us to forget the pros and cons of our actions that has led

America to the brink of an unprecedented depression to come after 2015.

The evidence is all around us. In fact, I recall an argument with my wife Suzanne, who is first generation American. I can recall the argument that we had just after I had written the chapter on generational wealth, in September, 2009. We had just come back from a hotel get-away when we were settling down back home. I noticed that my wife had thrown away a small piece of soap which to her did not mean anything but to me demonstrated how much we had changed from one generation to another just to be Americanized. What bothered me the most was that she threw away a shrunken down piece of soap, the same size as the ones we all have in our hotel rooms. When I questioned her about it, she said it was done and that was the reason for throwing it away. To my amazement the soap she threw away was the same size of soap that was okay at the hotel for us to use but was not okay for us to finish at home. If you are not a foreigner then you may not relate to this story. If you are, you know that this small bar of soap would be used up until it was gone. And my wife did not get it at first. The experience alone was shocking for me to see how far we have come being one generation apart from our lineage.

From the Irish migration to Staten Island, to the lucrative importation of slaves from Africa to America, we have forgotten the value of not wasting anything or taking our lives for granted. The baby boomers did a great job at raising the next generation after. They did a great job building America into what it is today, but where the baby boomers failed was at their greatest endeavor. For the most part, teaching their kids humility, morals, and values was where they fell short. Today, I look at Generation X, the future Digital Generation to come afterwards, and wondered how we got here, why our children are so lost. The answer lies in what you and I did after we became successful. Again the definition of success varies for different people. So let's define what I am talking about.

The baby boomers grew up in hardship and tough times, meaning, World War II and the Great Depression. Depending on when they were born, they all felt the residual effects in how their parents raised them. They knew how to value and appreciate the smallest things they had. They all grew up, became adults, and desired a better life for their children, like all parents do.

Baby boomers built and created wealth for themselves through real estate, careers, economic development, and education. They accomplished their goals and wanted like every parent to spoil their children with the luxuries of the fruits of their hard labor. They shelter their children, shower them with money, cars, homes, and jobs because they own the businesses for the most part. Along the way, they stopped teaching their children values that were important to the foundation of this great country and it became a greed infested give me/gimme mentality without having to earn it or work hard for it. Soon after the baby boomer's children grew up and became adults themselves wanting more and more of the good life their parents gave them.

By now, the value systems have faded away and that first generation of Americans are starting to have children of their own. Those children are part of that Generation X and future Digital Generation to come, all at a lost and without a purpose.

Now a new generation is born, of children raising children. A new generation of children being raised by television, sex symbols, sex ads, baggy pants-with no understanding of the history behind the phenomena.

Along the way, we have substituted money as a value system that can replace communicating with our children. We have spoiled them to death as grandparents with gifts and other monetary things that should never replace the love and affection that our children needed. Money replaced the attention our children wanted from us parents.

The nanny raised our children for us while we traveled the world, built our careers, and placed family values on the back burner. Money had substituted our responsibility to take care of our parents and grandparents in the home while passing on their wisdom to their grandchildren instead of sending them to a retirement home.

I attended a business conference for one of my network marketing companies a few years ago and I watched a training that was so powerful that I must share it with you because it is a good way of explaining what I just stated above in the simplest form. The example given was a visual concept on communication. The speaker was trying to make a point about what happens when we failed to be on one accord with the information that has been given to us to pass on to our downline organization. You actually can do this demonstration yourself.

If you take a can of Coca Cola or even Pepsi, as long as it is dark enough you can follow along. Have 10 to 15 cups of white clear glasses, filled half way with water. Start pouring the Coke or Pepsi into the first glass of water. Now watch how much darker it is with the drink you just poured in. Think of that dark Coke or Pepsi as information or communication you have just sent to your top leaders in your business or organization to be passed down to the rest of your staff or team. Now pass that information or glass of drink on to the next glass by pouring the first glass onto the second and the second onto the third, then the third on to the fourth, and so on until you reach the last one. See what happened?

Before you get even half way through all the glasses of water, you start to notice that the Coke is being diluted in front of your very eyes. You cannot see any signs that there was even a drop of Coke in the water from the previous glass.

The point of the demonstration[li] was to make sure your team or staff members have a clear line of communication from one source and not many rather than each person giving you a small piece of the information.

Now let's go back to the previous point that I was trying to make about what our ancestors gave up for us. By us, parents / baby boomers having given too much to our children without ever letting them know what it means to struggle or value hard work, we have actually diluted the mission or purpose for why our ancestors came to America for. Donny Deutsch from the hit show on CNBC called, *The Big Idea*[iii] wrote a book based on the same title as his show. In it, he makes a great statement, "And if you are a parent, don't rob your kids of the luxury of being hungry. It's something money can't buy."

To quote the great Andrew Carnegie in a similar statement he made; "The almighty dollar bequeathed to a child is an almighty curse. No one has the right to handicap his children with such a burden as great wealth."

In other words, we must make our children earn the right to access great wealth of teachings and disciplines at an early age. To go even further to understand what this has to do with being an entrepreneur, read Stanley and Danka's book, *The Millionaire Next Door*. These two gentlemen did an incredible job in explaining that there is a huge discrepancy between being rich and being wealthy. And this is one of the points I am trying to make you understand about money in this book. There is no real value in being content with making money at your job or small business and thinking that you are rich. Being rich is really a temporary state of finances.

How long can you keep up with your old habits before the money is gone should really be your number one concern. Learning how to create generational wealth and preserving it for future generations after you should be your number one priority. It should never be spent in one life time.

Your legacy should always be moving forward, economically speaking. Each time you leave your children's children to start over, it means that the lessons of wealth creation were never taught to you or passed on to the next generation. The only thing that you have been enjoying in life is the mentality of the rich and famous. And that does not last long.

I should point out that not every foreigner makes it big in America. Some still have to overcome the same trappings of success or discrimination. Many foreigners like my family came to America and relaxed. They followed the American way of a safe, secure job with benefits and retirement. They forget about the past or left it up to their children to pick up the baton that was left on the floor. Others are just content to have a job and food on the table, retire one day and go back home to die.

A large majority find themselves trap by the "Cycle of Oppression." The few that do make it in America have the hunger in them and they keep moving forward like the Nomads. They do not allow temporary success to become their resting stop. These foreigners go on to teach their children to open their own businesses.[liii] At a very young age you can find them working at their parents' store learning the family business so one day they too can take over and build a family of their own.

I have always been amazed how foreigners can come to America and understand the principles for which God put us on this earth-to be masters of all the land and not slaves of it. They have learned to build a business around their family that can support them rather than have a job that makes them slaves to the land and another master.

It is a harsh life when we, as foreigners, sacrifice so much to come to America only to find out that it is really not all that it is cracked up to be. Although foreigners may be free from the outright tyranny of their homeland, the struggle for survival is somewhat similar to the conditions they left behind. The only big difference is that they once could see their obstacles right in front of them while American struggles are subtle and deliberate. Many times hidden behind political walls and gridlock. It is even hard to tell sometimes when you have a roof over your head and a job. However, the life they live is much better than what most people have back home.

In 2013, President Obama fought an uphill battle to fix our immigration system. To create fair labor laws, equal rights, and provide citizenship for those who simply wish to have a piece of that American Dream. It is definitely not an easy one to win in states like Arizona, where Senator McCain is the spokesperson promoting the illegalization of immigrants, deportation, racial profiling, and maintaining of strict border patrols.

The irony of it all is that Americans need foreigners to clean out their toilets, cut their grass, and wait on them. These are the dirty jobs that Americans think are beneath them, even while they want to claim that immigrants are taking all of their jobs away. In fact, it is not true.

As I have said on my show, Voices4theVoiceless (V4DV), I have yet to see an immigrant, who could barely speak perfect English, working in corporate America as a CEO, CFO, VP, manager, or a supervisor of a Fortune 500 company. A cab driver, a cook, maintenance man, maid – these are the types of jobs they are often allowed to work for minimum wage. Many work two jobs without complaining to provide a better quality of life for their children who often become doctors, lawyers, business men and women, politicians. For them, this country is the land of opportunity. And that is why a small majority like Alan Greenspan[liv] understand the truth behind the lies. He went on record at the Senate Government Affairs Committee on "Federal Budget and Debt" to say, "immigrants are important to our economic growth. Americans will see a decline in the workforce by 2030 due to the retirement of baby boomers. Yet we want to miss treat these immigrant families who will become one day the faces of America."

THE CYCLE OF OPPRESSION

You would not notice it if you came to America as a foreigner but all Americans today came from a lineage that was once immigrant. It seems as though we have forgotten where we came from, since every immigrant who has come up the ranks as an American born citizen has in some way oppressed or discriminated against another person; someone who did not speak English well. This is undoubtedly the journey we all have gone through to claim our badge of freedom to the land of opportunity. You could almost call it our American hazing ritual.

As an observer of the world, particularly of the United States of America, I have watched how human beings oppress one another. In my thirty years living in this country, I have come to accept the fact that the cycle of oppression is an economic necessity. We may not all agree with it but that is how it has been done in America for hundreds of years. If you look at the world from a business perspective, you would agree with me that the cycle of oppression does follow in line with a Darwinism philosophy but more on an economic level for our survival.

Look for example at this simplified diagram[lv] of our human existence minus our civil and world wars. Every one hundred years or so, this diagram shifts and power is realigned again. Currently, Asians and Indians are in a league of their own where they are respected for their contribution to society and are highly respected for their intellect and what they bring to the fold. Asians bring manufacturing and Indians bring logistics and engineering. Whatever prejudice those two groups may face are probably on a smaller scale than the others. If I were to predict a form of prejudice they face in America, I would say it was internal.

Since the Jews were oppressed by the Nazi regime and Hitler's hatred, they have risen up to become an even stronger race of people. Their ordeal has bonded them to work together and create generations of wealthy elite people all across the country. The Jews

Cycle of Oppression in America

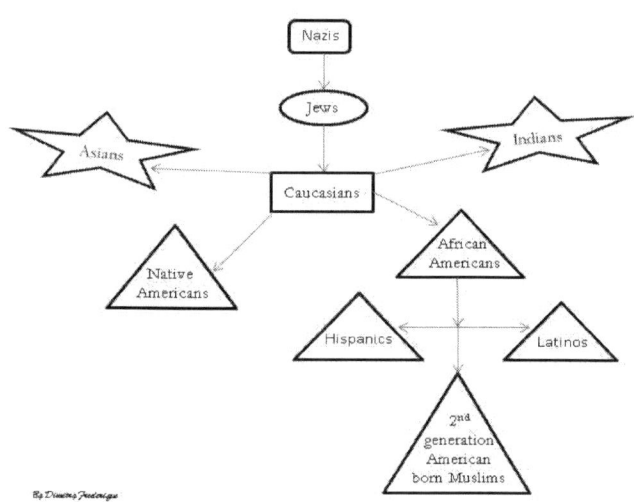

dominate our economy and the wealth that makes up much of present day America.

American-Irish Caucasian fought for their freedom from Europe and started a new world called the Americas. As America expanded and became more of an independent country, it needed slaves to work the land. There were not enough Native Americans to dominate and provide the labor force needed. Africa became the source for slaves and America developed into a civilization that required slaves as commerce grew even as it was the epitome of freedom, a New World. America later on became known as the Land of the Free, the home of the brave. Hence bringing in a new race of immigrants from Ireland who modernized America to what it is today.

The Jewish and Caucasian race have mixed over the past fifty years that you are not always able to separate the two races. Although descendants of Nazis, Jews, Caucasians, and African Americans have been mixed along the blood line, a new generation of children do not distinguish between race and cultural differences. That is why America is the only nation that cannot be identified as one race. We are a melting pot of races and descendants of immigrants.

African Americans were enslaved for more than 400 hundred years while building America's civilization to where it is today. They are people who have been oppressed and enslaved long after they have been set free. Today some have progressed and climbed the corporate structure of success in America. Having been given a chance to get an education, work, and provide for themselves financially, African Americans are slowly becoming owners of things once preserved for the elite race of white Americans.

African Americans, Hispanics, and Latinos are more or less equal to each other. We as a people do not own anything economically significant to contribute but that can all change with a new generation of Spanish speaking population. The last economic group that I see on the rise is a second generation of American born Muslims. The Native Americans currently have a hold on the conservation of land that they own and still stick together as a race. Since they don't normally deal with the outside cycle of oppression, they have maintained and preserved their culture and history.

As time went on, a new race was emerging, one who barely spoke a bit of English. Their population grew while Africans moved up the chain ladder of succession and claimed America as their homeland too. To America's surprise, Spanish Americans grew as a tight niche culture themselves and demanded the respect of all Americans by making Spanish the second largest speaking language in the world. Spanish Americans grew up and sought out more rights for themselves in the political world. By the 2016 Presidential election, the Spanish vote will probably determine who will become the next president of the United States of America. Hence the reason why both parties will heavily campaign to capture those votes.

As America went through yet another evolution, this time in the working class, a new educated, intelligent race that was once oppressed back home was now migrating to America seeking that same hope and opportunity that all previous generations of immigrants walked away from. Today, India is not only an emerging country but it is also the home for millions who have found their way to America via a work visa or international student pass. Half of that population is English speaking today. They have taken over the day to day work load of the American working class overseas. For a few pennies on the dollar, corporate America has depended on this new thriving economy to continue to provide them with record breaking profits year after year. Today just about everyone in corporate America is on the Indian band wagon for cheap labor.

Despite the tremendous progress that has been made in this country, efforts to manifest the principles upon which the country was truly founded, the wealthy and the powerful continue to create and utilize systems for oppression and exploitation.

For that reason alone we are in a different era where racism no longer works but money does. It is still the one thing that separates us all.

As technology increases, our global economy continues to grow rapidly. In exchange for quarterly profits, a new source of cheap labor must be found and oppressed at all cost. Hence a new cycle of oppression has begun and you are still working hard for 20th century ideals that have since been forgotten at the turn of the new millennium.

Have you ever once wondered where all that wealth and economic boom went over the past two decades? Where did all that dot com and real estate growth go after it was all said and done? Where did all that money go? As Jerry Maguire would say, "show me the money!" And gladly enough, all that money and wealth has moved on overseas, to the next deprived country. Money move electronically through cyberspace from country to country like a crowd wave around a stadium. From a click of the mouse on Wall Street to a phone call made hundreds of miles away, millions of dollars' worth of investments are transferred back and forth.

If you don't already know it, the wealthy are simply moving their money from country to country to find cheap labor. The cost of labor, goods, and services are determined from the stock exchanges every single day. Whether you are sleeping or awake, someone is determining your value as a commodity.

For example, have you ever pondered as to why jobs keep leaving America for countries like China, Japan, Africa, India, or even Haiti and other third world countries? Well, you can actually thank (or blame) Walther Reuther[lvi] at the same time for this problem. He gave Americans what they wanted over fifty years ago. You can basically label Reuther as one of the founding fathers for modern day labor laws that we have today. He pioneered the movement for the benefits you enjoy today such as better wages, forty hour work week schedules, better health care services, disability, unemployment benefits, and retirement packages like baby boomers' pensions.

For you to even begin to understand what happened to your US jobs, you first must understand what happened to the labor forces in the US over a hundred years ago.

If you can recall your middle school or high school history lessons, America thrived during the industrial revolution and with the emergence of the railroad industry. That was what really sparked the US job market. It also brought about harsh labor environments, unsanitary working conditions, and a workman's comp nightmare. Fast forward fifty or so years later comes Walther Reuther after the Great Depression with new ideas and a vision of how to improve the workforce by what he dubbed "social insurance." He fought long and hard over the years to bring about fair wages, vacation time, sick leave, and many other benefits we take for granted today.

By the 70s and 80s, Americans had a fair working environment with yearly increases in pay, bonuses, and other perks that came along with the formation of the union forces. Mr. Reuther eventually became a nightmare for big businesses and HR. He knew how to control the system and unite all the union employees to get what they wanted.

These were the days when unions had power over local, state, and presidential elections. Their votes mattered and they knew it. Corporate America eventually got smart and changed the game. They took back power over the unions and over their employees. What Walther Reuther had accomplished over the years became the driving force behind outsourcing of American jobs for cheaper labor.

In essence we became our own worst enemy. If you recall what I said about government jobs, America climbed the benefits ladder until there was no more money to be had. Corporate executives were tired of being squeezed out of their profits and they fought back. They dismantled these unions with threats of *Pension Dumping*, downsizing, layoffs, and outsourcing of jobs. And they did it *While America Aged* and kept on doing it to what you see today. Eventually it was no longer an issue of regaining control or cutting back. It was an issue of how much profits can be squeezed out of every employee. How much of a profit or bonus can these CEOs earn each quarter? If you recall after the government bailouts, CEOs gave themselves bonuses, for a job well done, even though we came so close to falling into another Great Depression.

This is when it became about greed and a revision to the cycle of oppression. Our systems realized that everyone in America were living up to the expectation of the Joneses and of course wanted more. Corporate America wanted more. Stock holders and foreign investors wanted more. Middleclass Americans wanted more. Even our children wanted more. Who else was there left to oppress? The Chinese and Japanese had control of all the jobs and manufacturing. The Indians had all of the outsourcing jobs with the help of other third world countries. Who was really left?

Our systems realized that African Americans, other minorities, middleclass, and the poor do not really have much to contribute even though African Americans are the most consumable race of them all. So who else was there to pick from? This issue was around the same time that the immigration problems were becoming bigger issues for Americans. Who else can we blame for shipping our jobs away? We were not going to blame ourselves.

Of course it had to be the immigrants taking away American jobs. As I have stated earlier, Senator McCain took the lead in trying to make sure that foreigners were not coming in to take the last remaining jobs it had left. It is also during that same time period that America's family values had gone down the drain. High school dropout was at an all-time high and so were teenage pregnancies. Family values and morals were all a thing of the past.

It is my belief that our system eventually came up with one solution for all of these problems, including the shortage of slave labor. Instead of having an open door policy of foreigners, coming in to America and becoming a statistical success story, middleclass Americans moving up economically, or the poor keep being a burden to society, why not just oppress all of them? Let them turn on each other. Keep them in the same economic position that they are in right now. Let them keep chasing the bling, blings. Let them keep wanting to be celebrities and superstars. Let them keep chasing that American Dream, the life of the rich and fabulous.

As I have stated in previous chapters, our systems do know how to control us as test subjects. I strongly believe that our current system does understand how to create a new cheaper labor force by way of the next generation. Instead of letting foreigners go through the same cycle of oppression that has been tradition, why not just dumb them down over a period of time. If you think about it, it does make sense. It does explain why this country is moving last in education: mathematics, reading, writing, and science. It does explain why this country allows a generation to keep prostituting their babies for governmental benefits.

If you are still wondering what children having children has to do with entrepreneurship, here is the connection: America is no longer the number one superpower country that it used to be. We have been letting things go unresolved since the Great Depression. Every major issue has been pushed along for the next generation to deal with. By 2015, the biggest issue our government will have to deal with is the baby boomers and their retirement packages. Our government and the rest of corporate America are far behind in their commitment to pay these baby boomers. So much so that I think they have devise a plan to entice our youth to get into the work force early.

Since 2011, I have been counting down on V4DV to our financial meltdown. The system cannot afford children spending between eight and twelve years in the school system getting an education. If you do the math, that is four years of high school, four more years for a college education, and possibly another two to four years of grad school afterwards. Hence the reason they must shorten that time by offering them a place to work, as I have previously stated in the first half of part one. That is why so many older people are also being laid off. Our systems realize that they need our children to be out in the real world, working rather than wasting their time going to school. This action will compensate for the baby boomers low ratio of retirees to the number of people working.

You have to remember that back in the day, for every one retiree, there were three people working. Today it is more like one person working for every three retiree. You don't need to do the math to realize that this is America's biggest Ponzi scheme ever created. And like any other scam in the world, you have to have a flood of new people contributing to the scam for it to continue working. Our systems need more workers. A cheaper, uneducated group of employees who have gotten trapped by their lifestyle.

If you take a look at *Pension Dumping* by Fran Hawthorne, you would realize that the industrial revolution was an introduction; the first opportunity for the working class to be enslaved through a labor force hidden behind a demand for skilled workers who could lay down railroad tracks. Once their time was up, a pension plan was concocted to push these workers out of the picture. The scam worked well until the baby boomers were born because now they had a new problem in their hands since 1946 and 1963. The largest generation ever born only produced 1.5 kids on average. To compensate again for the lack of working age people when boomers retire, our systems made it possible for Generation X to keep having kids without setting aside a real future for them. And the cycle continues to bring us to what you see today with what I call the Digital Generation.

The two fatal mistakes that our systems made in the process contributed to this epidemic. First, our systems never accounted for our utopian society to interact economically or culturally the way it has. We are indeed an interracial race of American pop culture in the 21st century. The once perfect and elite race in society has been infiltrated with the same decline of morals and family values too. The system never accounted for America's infatuation with entertainment and fame would bring strangers together.

Second, we thought that through this process, we would have the best of the best children continue on to get those high degrees. And the future generation of kids going to college right now are starting to realize that it is not worth the headache. Many are following suit and going straight into the work force while others are just following their dreams of making it big in Hollywood. This problem creates another dilemma for the IRS. They are not collecting enough in taxes first to pay back the money they "borrowed" from the baby boomers' pension, let alone have enough money to give them a retirement check each month. Second, the IRS does not have enough working educated people to take on these higher paying hi-tech jobs that President Obama is pushing for from his State of the Union Addresses. Third, even though more students will come on to the work force early, it is still not enough money being collected to compensate for the sheer amount of baby boomers retiring at 10,000 a day. Fourth, the IRS never planned for a boom and bust era, high unemployment rates, deflation, the devaluing of our currency, the fiscal cliff, two wars, and many more problems on the horizon to come.

Were you able to keep up? I hope you are starting to wake up and realize that being an entrepreneur may not be a bad idea after all. Last but not least, what our systems have allowed to happen to our children in the past few years will prove to be more damaging than the birth of the baby boomers. The baby boomers grew up creating the society we see today. They also inherited a lot of wealth from their parents after the Great Depression. Generation X has nothing really to show for their success, except what has been passed down to them.

Worse than that, our systems think they can fix the retirement loophole by enticing our youth to have more babies without forgetting that was the big problem from the start. Malcolm Gladwell explained in *Outliers* how society had to adapt to an unexpected flow of overcrowded children in the classrooms. You cannot predict how many kids each generation will have and you cannot try to balance it out like China did with their one child per family policy.

This is why our pyramid scheme, what you call a J.O.B, does not work. You cannot account for every person living, dying, or being born to replace the next coming generation of people. If anything, we are setting ourselves to repeat the same mistakes of the baby boomer generation. Only this time, your children will be born into an even greater depression than the one we recovered from after 1929.

AMERICA
- THE MELTING POT-

Wikipedia defines the word Utopia as "an unrealistic ideal that is impossible to achieve."

When we think of the word Utopia, we think of this universal world where all races come to live together. America seems to be the only country that accepts all races to come in and make something of yourself. But is that really true when the outside world sees America with all its glamour and exotic life style as an ideal place to come and make something of yourself? In fact, we live in a very segregated world base on class, culture, and economic status.

Unfortunately for those immigrants, the success rate is very low. So low, in fact, that only a few will make it big in business right away. Those who fail to make it find themselves working hard, long hours, and maybe even a second job just to make ends meet. This was the case of a Portuguese speaking custodian that I met a few years ago in a medical establishment. I was introduced to her by a mutual friend, who informed me that she was cheated out of her overtime pay on many occasions. Sad to say, I was not surprised since her story was like many others I have read of or heard about in the past who were Jews or Greeks that had migrated to America. It is part of the cycle of oppression they all must face to give birth to a new generation of American citizens who will one day become small business owners in our communities.

Upon arrival to the US, many immigrants inevitably fail to recognize

America's biggest secret until they are settled in their comfort zone five to ten years later. And that secret becomes an epiphany of a life time once they realize that the opportunity is really them; the same one so many people had deemed to be the American Dream back home.

The real truth is that America is really not the land of opportunity. It is the land of poverty. In order for America to stay number one and maintain its legacy, to continue to be the Mecca for all of those who are oppressed and persecuted, America has to live up to its reputation as being a dominate super power. The truth of the matter is that America would really be nothing without its slaves and today without its immigrant workers who are coming here to seek out a better life.

As I write this, millions of immigrants are sacrificing their lives, risking everything so they can pursue the American Dream.

For most of them, America is the safe haven. It is the answer to their struggles and the end to their poverty. Surprisingly enough, America has a different plan for our fellow first generation immigrants who come to America.

Simply put, Americans really need immigrants to come to this country so they can keep the cycle of oppression and wealth going. American ingenuity is dead. There have not been that many new innovative ideas created by an American for almost thirty years; certainly not one that has created millions of jobs for people.

With the exception of Mark Zuckerberg of Facebook, which is a widely held stock today, I don't count internet base companies from the last decade as job creators. A large majority of them do not create that many jobs to speak of. Companies like Amazon, which operates out of a large warehouse for distribution of their products, have fought against paying taxes because they considered themselves to be a cloud base company.

Needless to say, companies are hiring illegal immigrants to work in America every day. It is a big political game that is being played out in Congress and you, the American public.

I've seen the hatred that Americans have for immigrants because they are "taken away our jobs." What we are really listening to is propaganda. Folks in my years of living in America, I have yet to see an American dying and fighting with all arms crying out to keep their precious position of being a dish washer, a peasant, a maid, a janitor, a house keeper, fruit picker, a security guard, or a cab driver. So when you hear Americans crying about how immigrants are taking all of their jobs please understand that it is clearly a lie.

What I have concluded over the years is that the older generations must oppress the more recent generation of immigrants who come to America in search of a better way of life. That is the vicious cycle that is our culture; at least the American culture that I have come to know for the past thirty years.

What is really going on is the evolution of American society since our independence from England. It has been that way for centuries and it will continue to be that way for centuries to come. And if you are still baffled by what I have written, then you need to ask your government some serious questions as to why they allow immigrants certain rights under the radar.

As a past identity theft specialist, I know that the government openly allows immigrants to use your personal identity to work jobs that you and I would not want to do. And they hide behind red tape to even get one single law put in place.

As of 2013, President Obama has passed stricter laws in an attempt to hunt down cybercriminals. Nevertheless, with all the technologies we have to spy on people and process employee information digitally, our systems are telling us that they cannot flag anomalies in their databases? And why would they, when businesses are already paying them chump change or under the table.

The best method left is to allow immigrants to work illegally and have them do all the grunt work that you do not want to do. Meanwhile, they can avoid paying out benefits like legal Americans do. That is why your credit card company will allow someone to charge items under your name when it is not even you. That is why they offer you easy access mini keychain credit cards that can easily be stolen. That is why the government will allow your children or babies to become victims of identity theft without raising a red flag. It's crazy when you hear a five year old already has a house, a car, several credit cards, or bills under their name. That is why two people with the same identity or social security number can work two different jobs with conflicting time stamps and have taxes be collected from both people until one person does not pay them anymore. The only time it is a problem is when the government, i.e. the IRS, does not get its share of the pie. And guess who they really coming after? You, the victim!

As the cycle of oppression continues to spread worldwide, understand that our government and big businesses are making deals with foreign countries called "Free Trade" agreements that allow our jobs to be sent overseas in exchange for taking on our US debts. China owns us and so does the other major super powers because America has been declared too big to fail.

I did a four part series on the subject at V4DV.com that you can watch as well as another show entitled, "A Bankrupt Country will Always Lead to Chaos". It speaks of who actually owns the United States of America.

Aside from my show, you can also check out David C. Johnston's book about the *Free Lunch* this great country of ours serves to foreign countries in an attempt to retain friendly allies on foreign policy and free trade. I will come back to this subject in part 2 of chapter 6.

The incentives to do business overseas are irresistible to foreign leaders who face high unemployment numbers in their own country and who's people are living in poverty with no economic stability in site. All of a sudden, you look like a hero or a savior, when a wealthy businessman or woman calls you up to offer you the deal of a life time. Who in their right mind would not take the deal as president of a poor country?

Of course, with every deal comes the "what's in it for me?" In return for the cheap labor, many of these big businesses are asking for huge tax breaks, write offs, tax shelters, and many more loopholes that protects them from having to ever pay out one dime to the US government.

Let me remind you that several of these working environments are nothing more than sweatshops. This is why it is so lucrative for corporate America to move their manufacturing plants offshore and still increase their profits. And for the next thirty to fifty years, they will continue to strip these innocent workers of their freedom, pride, and dignity, just so they can feed their families. It is slave labor at its finest. Once they are done, they will simply move on to the next country, desperately searching for an answer.

The only reason why it will take between thirty and fifty years for things to change is that someone like a Walther Reuther needs to be born to fight for their economic freedom. It will take a lot of education, training, and unionization of jobs before these folks can see any fair working condition, pay raises, a salary, and many other benefits that American workers get to enjoy. Once these laws are in place, many of these businesses will move shop to find the next willing country.

To make matters worse, many of these developing countries don't even have laws to protect children and adults from harsh working conditions that was once the environment of the industrial revolution. Until someone speaks up and demands better working conditions, regulate the workforce with certain standards, the cycles of oppression will continue on.

As demand for products spike, expect more people to die from injuries, infections, and chemical fumes coming out of these new high tech machineries than ever before.

And the cycle will continue on and on and on, until someone wakes up and sees what's happening to these workers. This same scenario has already taken place in countries like China. For the past fifteen years, while Americans were enjoying their economic growth, the Chinese government was mobilizing its aging population of farmers to a more modern civilization in prefab cities. They developed malls, houses, corporate jobs – all this just to lure in a new generation of young workers similar to what American businessmen did at the start of the 20th century. As you can see, history keeps on repeating itself over and over again. Instead of railroads in the 21st century, it is tall skyscrapers.

The images you are looking at was taken by the Associated Press from The Wall Street Journal website in 2013, showing what's left of these "Nail Houses" as they are called of people who refuse to move out of the way. Instead of forcing them out developers just built around them.

WHERE DOES HATRED & SELF DESTRUCTION COME FROM?

Why is it so hard for humanity to move forward in peace; for all of us to work together for the common good of mankind? The answer to this question stems from our history and three unlikely philosophies that I have put together in this chapter to explain why we are hateful to one another and practice such self-destructive behaviors that prevent us from ever becoming successful in life.

On September 9, 2009, I got an interesting history lesson from my good friend Linda L. Johnson, who was an insurance sales rep at the time. She shared with me her story of having meet a Haitian and Vietnamese couple who were getting insurance from her. All the husband could talk about was how great Haiti was at one time. For those who do not know, on January 1st, 1804, Haiti made history by being the first black country to gain its independence. It was once a wealthy country, until it was robbed of its resources and destroyed by Napoleon Bonaparte. Our people were warriors who fought for their freedom but the price we paid for our freedom was our financial stability.

On V4DV, I have done a show entitled, Qui Probleme Ayiti? /What Is Haiti's Problem? It turns out that the very thing that freed us has since enslaved us till this day. African Americans slavery would have the opposite affect which I will explain later on.

It was around the time that I was reading Malcolm Gladwell's *Outliers* that I got a very interesting lesson on American history. In chapter six of his book, Gladwell speaks of the origin of aggression and later chapters about accents. (Please read the book for more details.) When it comes to aggression, we do not need to look any further than the ancestry of your grandparents, to whether or not they were born in the North or in the South.

Studies showed that people who tend to have come from the South are quick to get angry or be more aggressive than those who are born in the North. When it comes to accents, we can relate differences in how we speak.

Gladwell suggest the best way to lose an accent is to be far removed from the origin of that accent. So a person born with a Southern accent can simply move to the North and will eventually lose that accent.

And this is how these three schools of thought came together for me, to develop this theory on the stagnant progression of black America today.

It feels as though I have heard that specific question all my life, about why black America cannot seem to progress any further than where we were put on this earth to be.

To give you a clear answer, I must first start off where I left Linda's story about Haiti. Haitians seems to have a fight in them like no other race and it stems back to the day of our independence.

Reading Gladwell's philosophy on aggression made me realized that we are so different from any other country because we were the only one who did successfully fight for our freedom. And you can compare that to American slavery. There is something to be proud of once you fought for your freedom versus when it was handed down to you. It is a power that cannot be taken away from you. It is in your blood line forever. I see it even in myself.

Don't get me wrong, I am well aware of what leaders like Frederick Douglas, Harriet Tubman, Booker T. Washington, Malcolm X, Dr. Martin Luther King, Jr. and others did for African Americans. The one flaw, that all these great leaders have, is that they were not the ones who ended slavery.

White America ended slavery with the Emancipation Proclamation of 1863. Black America would have never been where it is today if President Abraham Lincoln did not hand us our freedom versus fighting for it ourselves. President Lincoln actually did us a disservice the day he handed us our freedom. There is a greater sense of pride when you fight for a cause and win. It brings you greater meaning and a greater sense of achievement. President Lincoln took away our pride, our freedom, our hope of accomplishing something great. Something that all African Americans, even to this day, could have held their heads up proudly to say we did it ourselves. It is that same pride that Haitians still talk about today.

Think about what happened after slavery. We still had to keep on fighting for our freedom. The piece of paper really did not mean anything to us. After slavery was officially abolished, white men still dominated the world economic system. It was not like a truths meeting where white slave mastered sat down with blacks and said this is our concession. This is the terms in which we are willing to surrender. In return we are willing to give you this piece of land or territory. Nothing like that happened. Instead, we were the ones still begging after we were emancipated. We were the ones asking, what do we do now and how do we feed ourselves and our children? Even to this day, we see the cycle of oppression still living on because we never owned anything to begin with even our freedom. It was all handed down to us.

Stanley and Danko of *Millionaire Next Door* have stated that the same is true for American born citizens with a sense of entitlement. So much has been given to them that they never had to fight to get it.

Overtime, white Americans have become complacent as well in their success, when they simply pass it on to their children without having them work hard for it or appreciate the opportunities they were born with. It is for that reason America needs new immigrants. As baby boomers retire in the coming years, the transfer of wealth will shift once again, to a new generation that is not ready to receive an inheritance. All they will do is squander over materialistic things, things that society tells them they need to have.

So why are African Americans still more aggressive than whites? Well, the display of aggression that you see today is true display of what happens when freedom loses its value.

Instead of fighting the enemy, we took out our aggression on each other. There was no self-pride any more. We were forced to look at our skin color for the first time and fight for our individual survival. In hindsight if you take a look back at slavery and the industrial age that was the very things that drove commerce in America and would later on economically strip African Americans of their freedom and reenlist middle class Americans back to slave labor. Instead of becoming farmers or moving to the North, as many of us did, millions more have stayed behind to settle for a paycheck. The majority of African Americans are still conditioned to the past based on what our ancestors did. And that is choosing to remain in the deep South where hatred and racism still exist today. Eventually we, as a people, turned to black on black crime and violence. Similar to Gladwell's explanation of accents, those who stayed behind and never ventured off North still carried on that slave mentality that we see in the 21st century. It is for that reason oppression still lives on from generation to generation, like a never ending family feud.

Like the family feuds in Harlan, Kentucky, Southern blacks still to this day cannot separate from the environment in which they grew up in. Those who did manage to move up North learned new behaviors and got rid of their slave mentality. They started their own businesses or learned new skills.

What I have learned from reading *Outliers* and being reminded of my Haitian ancestry from Linda is that hatred and self-destruction are a generational curse that can be unlearned through education.

The only thing that I know that I have control over is my mind. If you do not have the inert desire to be free, if you do not have the desire to actively want more out of life, to want a better future for yourself and your legacy, will you pay the ultimate price for remaining still. You have to constantly be evolving like everything else in this world, this universe. You have to feed your mind on a regular basis with positive stuff. Not just when it pleases you or someone says read that book or attend this seminar with me. You have to force yourself to do something totally different from what you are use to doing. To achieve greatness, you must get out of your comfort zone. That is a fact that cannot be ignored on any level. No one is going to do it for you.

One thing is for sure, racism and prejudice will never end because like the air we breathe in, it's all around us. We cannot escape it or block it from entering our home. I don't believe hatred will ever go away. It more or less gets transformed or blends in with the rest of society as time changes.

What happened to the white American born and raised as a second or third generation Ku Klux Klan (*KKK*)? Where did they go? Nowhere, a matter of fact these people are all around us. They are some of the elite few that we interact with every day at work. Some of them can be found on the top floors of their corporate headquarters. It's the same headquarters that we go into each day trying to climb that corporate ladder. They are the same ones we salute to in the military. They are the same ones we shake hands with and they smile back at us. They are the same ones who we address politely, with whom we use phrases like, "yes sir," "no ma'am," "thank you, boss." "Can I work/have some extra hours boss?" "Thanks boss for the promotion." For those who have forgotten the price our ancestors paid for your freedom, let me remind you. "Yes Master," "no thank you Mistress," "no Master," "thank you Master." "Master can you spare a dime so that I can feed my family?" "Master, I have done a good job for you for the past twenty years out in the field, can I be your house slave since Kunta Kinte is dead now?"

Slave masters did not go anywhere. They just gave you a dollar bill and an office space to make you think you are still free. If you are Caucasian, please don't think you are excluded from this self-hatred or destruction, too. They also see you as traders, for having failed to preserve the white race. Unfortunately, you are just a victim of circumstance. Today we are all victims to economic slavery. There are no exceptions based on race, gender, or ethnicity.

Those who have rebuked racism have separated from the Klan (see Johnny Lee Clary's interviews on youTube.com) but not all have changed the error of their ways, especially in the deep south. We never saw the face of KKK members. They too have transformed and transitioned just like you and I have adapted in the 21st century. Their hatred has not gone away. You really cannot get rid of them that easily. Their hatred has evolved over the decades.

Don't forget that this country became a true melting pot of interracial marriages and new born babies. While the KKK was once worried about blacks and whites mixing races, they now have to deal with everyone mixing and cross breading. There are more interracial marriages of Asians, Caucasians, African Americans, Jewish, Spanish, Latinos, etc. than there has ever been before since the 1960s and 1970s. In fact a Pew Research Center study[lvii] shows that nearly 15 percent of U.S marriages are indeed interracial as of 2008.

And that's a great thing, because it shows that we are embracing our cultural differences and making race nonexistent. At least the younger generation are. Let's not forget that this number may very well be greater for non-married couples living in America with children. Nevertheless, this fact alone has angered the KKKs. If anything, their hatred goes out to anyone who has "tainted" their race. Mainly white America forgot that the KKK's premise was based on preserving the white race-white supremacy. Today America is so mixed that our DNA is really a representation of the United States of America, a Utopian society.

Only when we all have come into agreement to put a stop to hatred or end racism, will it actually stop. But it takes all of us (the human race) to come into agreement. It cannot be a selected few that decides and agrees that change is good but nothing else happens. It is for that reason we must all do our part to make sure that our people rise above mediocrity; to ensure that we teach our children that "*Success Runs in Our Race.*[lviii]"

We do not have to watch what the Ku Klux Klan did to understand that racism still exists today. Just look at how corporate America treats black CEOs. Actually, it is what you don't see in the media's eye. Corporate America is so scared of how others would react to knowing that a none white person is at the helm of the CEO position of well-respected companies that they keep it hush-hush (American Express, Symantec Corporation, McDonald's USA, Merrill Lynch & Co, Citigroup Inc., Xerox Corporation, and Aetna Inc. to name a few). They've all had a black CEO at one point or another. It's another way of discouraging minorities by never allowing them to see and dream that they too can reach the mountain top of some great companies.

Young minority kids have nothing worthy to inspire them in the corporate world to say when I grow up, I want to be the CEO of such and such company. Instead they are left with limited resources.

They have basketball, baseball, or football players as role models. Simply because that is all the skills society labels them to be good at in their community. Never once have they been allowed to see success outside of a basketball court or a baseball field. Black CEOs are hardly ever shown in front of the TV addressing their employees at a boardroom meeting or during a commercial featuring them. What respectable images are put in front of tomorrow's children that say you can become somebody great? That you too can run that Fortunate 500 company one day too.

Where are those images and examples for our future grand children to see? They don't exist. When I ask tomorrow's parents to rise above their poverty and broken down dreams and innovate their children, it is to give their children examples to work towards. You have no right to tell them; "well I never amount to anything. Your mother, sisters, and brothers have never amounted to nothing at all. Your great, great grandparents before us did not become anyone special. So it is okay not to set your expectation high because you too will never amount to nothing at all." Each time you speak those words or thoughts into their heads, you are setting your own family generations back.

As Pastor Matthew Thompson would say, you have allowed the baton to be dropped if you do not set an example. You have failed not only yourself but your children's children ability to pass their baton forward to the next generation; leaving them to be lost in the world and to carry your curse forward.

Our words speak life into our children. And if our words are not all positive, our children will forever be broken from the inside out. They will grow up to become adults with damaged goods. Now it will take three times more effort to repair the damage caused by your negative words or thoughts as a parent than saying something positive. Imagine each negative word we say to our children about success and achievement were feathers tossed in the winds. And you are assigned the task of retrieving every single one of them back, would you be able to do it? Never let a day go by without speaking life into them, inspiring them to be great, making them discover their purpose on Earth, and telling them to reach for the stars.

Have you ever been bothered by the news when you hear that high school students are committing hate crimes or committing suicide because someone on Facebook said mean things about them? Well you don't have to look far for the causes of these sad stories all across the country. It is really the reality of what's going on at home. No one is around the home often enough to say I love you to that child. No one is around to tell them they are beautiful. No one is around really to do some serious parenting. All in all these kids are just lost souls because someone along the way did not think it was important to speak life into that child. Either work or that parent's personal life took precedence over that child's life. And that is why you see the end results of hatred being spread and the senseless destruction of lives being lost at such a young age. The freedom that entrepreneurship offers you does make a difference. A few hours a day last a life time of memories never forgotten. It is those memories that will be passed on to their children's children one day.

Coming soon...

PART 2

"EVERYTHING STARTS AND ENDS WITH A BUSINESS"

* CHAPTERS

(5) Baby Boomer Generation
1946 – 1963

(6) Let's Blame the Politicians

(7) Network Marketing

(8) What does it mean to be an Entrepreneur?

* Chapters are subject to change.

ABOUT THE AUTHOR

This is Dimitry Frederique's second published book and first business book. He is the CEO and founder of Poetic Imagery in Motion, a subsidiary of Frederique Media Productions and Frederique Capital, the parent company. He also produces and owns a biweekly financial educational show geared towards business owners, network marketers, and those of like mindedness online. Voices4theVoiceless (V4DV) is an extension of Why Entrepreneurship? What is IT All About? since January of 2011. You can follow his show on http://Voices4theVoiceless.com; on Twitter: @V4DV; http://facebook.com/frederique.capital or http://Facebook.com/Voices4theVoiceless. Also like and befriend the official page on FB - http://Facebook.com/whyentrepreneurship and let us start a dialogue online.

His love for business goes back to his childhood days as he would sit at home and contemplate witty inventions. In 1999, he took a leap of faith and started his entrepreneurial journey as a computer technician and a philosopher. In his spare time, he ventured into the world of network marketing and loved it.

For the past twenty years he has traveled the country and has been trained by the best of the best in the network marketing field. It was through network marketing, in fact, that he also fell in love with personal development and gained a greater understanding of business and a growing desire to become an entrepreneur one day.

Over the years, he spent hours upon hours discussing some of the key issues concerning job security and the future of the middle class with his friends and colleagues in the business world. It was those conversations that led him to become a vocal voice in the community about business ownership and the importance of owning something for yourself. However it was not until he got married was he then inspired to finally put his years of experience into words.

An intellectual argument with his wife would spark the question in his head, why is it that everyone does not get it? Why does the world not understand the importance of leaving an inheritance to our children's children? Why is it that only a small portion of us (less than 3%) realize that everything starts and ends with a business? That the world runs on a global platform that is operated by business owners and entrepreneurs. Since that day in 2008, it became his quest to educate the world and let everyone know why entrepreneurship is the answer and the solution to our financial problems facing us all in the 21st century.

ENDNOTES / REFERENCES

---

i

Video clip of Oprah Winfrey at the 25th Annual Daytime Emmy Awards in 1998 http://archives.voices4thevoiceless.com Pg. 7

ii

Antz produced by DreamWorks Animation in 1998. Pg. 13

iii

Finding Nemo produced by Pixar Animation Studios in 2003. Pg. 13

iv

Lion King produced by Walt Disney Pictures in 1994 http://www.imdb.com/title/tt0110357/ Pg. 13

v

Similar references can be found online by Derrick Carpenter via his blog site called "Start With The End In Mind" http://30secondcommute.blogspot.com/2010/05/do-you-know-difference-between-work-and.html Pg. 21

vi

"Crown Biblical Financial Study, Life Group Manual" by Crown Ministries, Pg.: 27

vii

As of 2011, PPL is now called LegalShield. And is now owned by MidOcean Partners. The CEO is Rip Mason Pg. 29

viii

MSNBC "Nightly News" with Brian Williams aired 10/16/2009 David Heim's website http://wheelchairrecycler.org Pg. 32

ix
Heroes was created by Tim Kring and ran on NBC for four years. http://en.wikipedia.org/wiki/Heroes_%28TV_series%29 Pg. 35

x
Scripture passages taken from the NIV. Pg. 44

xi
Pastor Matthew Thompson is the senior pastor at Jubilee Christian Church in Mattapan, MA Pg. 61

xii
No Condition Is Permanent! by Rene Godefroy - Rene shares his life story of how he came to America and sought out his dreams of becoming a motivational speaker. I had a chance to meet him in 2002. Pg. 83

xiii
Go to V4DV Archives to see actual footage of this experiment taking place. http://archives.v4dv.com Pg. 97

xiv. Verizon charges family over $18,000 for phone bill" http://www.boston.com/business/articles/2010/04/30/family_provider_far_apart_over_nearly_18000_phone_bill/?page=full Pg. 102

xv
Psychologist Dr. Michael Shermer, editor of Skeptics magazine, explains how our brain can sometime deceive us. http://www.msnbc.msn.com/id/38154937/ns/dateline_nbc/ the show was originally aired on Dateline NBC. Pg. 106

xvi

This was the same thing that happened to the railroad workers during the industrial revolution. Get them in while they are young and ship them out when they get old. Pg. 120

xvii In Outliers, Malcolm Gladwell reference that it takes on average about 10,000 hours or 10 years for anyone to master a skill successfully. Pg. 122

xviii

On October 15, 2009 Associated Press Writer Stephen Ohlemacher, wrote an article entitled, "No Social Security hike, could boost new payments" in response to Social Security Administration decision not to keep up with the cost-of-living increases for 2010 Pg. 129

http://www.newschannel10.com/global/story.asp?s=11322929

xix

February 19, 2013, Pres. Obama goes on a speaking tour to fight for government employees who might lose their jobs over sequester reform. Major cutbacks are expected across the board if agreement is not reached with the Republican Party. Pg. 130

xx
This is how the system views its employees. "Stubbornly high unemployment is viewed as the missing link in the economy's recovery from its worst recession in 70 years." ... "Since the start of the recession in December 2007, the number of unemployed people has risen by 7.6 million to 15.1 million, the Labor Department said. While the decline in payrolls has moderated from early this year, companies are still not hiring on a wide scale, likely waiting for a signal that the economic recovery is sustainable." "U.S. Sept non-farm payrolls plunge 263,000" - Reporting by Lucia Mutikani; Editing by Andrea Ricci On October 2, 2009
http://www.worldslastchance.com/prophecy-in-news/us-sept-non-farm-payrolls-plunge-263000.html Pg. 132

xxi
A great dramatization of that is seen in the movie Margin Call directed by J.C. Chandor in 2011. Pg. 132

xxii
Gov. Patrick threatens to Boycott the Hyatt Hotel Corp. on September 2009. Pg. 134

http://www.boston.com/business/articles/2009/09/24/govern or_threatens_a_hyatt_boycott/

xxiii
A 2009 report states that the Obama administration's housing rescue "was not designed to address foreclosures caused by unemployment, which now appears to be a central cause of nonpayment," "Foreclosure Epidemic Reaching More Expensive Homes"http://money.usnews.com/money/blogs/the-home-front/2009/10/16/foreclosure-epidemic-reaching-more-expensive-homes Pg. 140

xxiv
Famous quote by Jim Rohn, an entrepreneur and an internationally known motivational speaker who has since pass in 2009. His audio CD is called, *Building Your Network marketing Business* Pg. 150

xxv
Japanese call this "karoshi" Article is taken from Business Insider, "15 Seriously Disturbing Facts About Your Job" by Alyson Shontell. http://www.businessinsider.com/disturbing-facts-about-your-job-2011-2?op=1   pg. 158

xxvi
A Yahoo Finance article "Some Firms Struggle to Hire Despite High Unemployment" gives a better picture of the unemployment scenario many faced. Pg. 162
http://finance.yahoo.com/news/pf_article_110277.html

xxvii Pension Dumping by Fran Hawthorne, pg. 168

xxviii
Pension Benefit Guaranty Corporation (PBGC) was created by the Employee Retirement Income Security Act to protect the pensions of participants in private benefit pension plans in case those companies went bankrupt. Pg. 169

xxix
A Ride on the Subway was the poem that I wrote in high school to express this view. This poem is not included in the first volume of Pages from My Heart. Pg. 174

xxx
Kiyosaki has stated that, "If people do not learn about money, they can end up exchanging their freedom for a paycheck-for a steady job and enough money to pay their bills."- Pg. 38, *Rich Dad's Conspiracy of the Rich – The 8 New Rules of Money*   Pg. 185

xxxi
Lindsey Piegza a financial economist who was interviewed on CNBC on 3/12/2013 hit it right on the money as she echoed the same sentiments about the value of a college education today.

http://video.cnbc.com/gallery/?play=1&video=3000153912&source=internal|promo|headerunit|&par=internal#eyJ2aWQiOiIzMDAwMTUzOTY2IiwiZW5jVmlkIjoiTzRsVk5XNVdyV0l1ZjdMOXlRTjdKdz09IiwidlRhYiI6InRyYW5zY3JpcHQiLCJ2UGFnZSI6IiIsImdOYXYiOlsiqBMYXRlc3QgVmlkZW8iXSwiZ1NlY3QiOiJVUyIsImdYWdlIjoxLCJzeW0iOiIiLCJzZWFyY2giOiIifQ== Pg. 188

xxxii
On March 30, 2013, The Wall Street Journal published an article estimating that 284,000 of college graduates are working minimum-wage jobs and another 37,000 have a graduate degree or more. Pg. 188
http://blogs.wsj.com/economics/2013/03/30/number-of-the-week-college-grads-in-minimum-wage-jobs/

xxxiii
They wrote *The Millionaire Next Door: The Surprising Secrets of America's Wealthy* in 1998. These 2 men have studied the lives of the affluent and what they actually spend their money on. Pg. 190

xxxiv
Robert Kiyosaki's *Rich Dad's Conspiracy of the Rich-The 8 New Rules of Money*, this book goes into greater details on the topic. Pg. 194

xxxv
She interviewed 4 students from the graduating class of 2009 in a broadcast called *"Out of School, Out of Work."* This interview is a far cry from what the average college graduate is left with - a school bag of broken promises and a trail of debt.
http://www.cbsnews.com/stories/2010/06/09/eveningnews/

main6566004.shtml?tag=cbsnewsTwoColUpperPromoArea Pg. 201

xxxvi

(V4DV) is a financial and educational show on business that I have been doing since 2011. http://Voices4theVoiceless.com Pg. 202

xxxvii

Money is not taught in schools. Schools focus on scholastic and professional skills, but not financial skills. This explains how smart bankers, doctors, and accountants who earned excellent grades in school may still struggle financially all their lives." by Robert Kiyosaki – this quote was taken from an advertisement for Rich Dad Workshop on October 7, 2009 in the Boston Metro newspaper. Pg. 206

xxxviii

He currently plays for the New York Knicks in 2013 after having played for 6 other franchises in the course of his 17 year career in the NBA. http://en.wikipedia.org/wiki/Marcus_Camby Pg. 207

xxxix

Statistically speaking most players are broke after 5 years in retirement. http://cdn.mediatakeout.com/21738/study-60-of-nba-players-are-broke-after-5-years-of-retirement.html Pg. 207

xl

Other players like Ray Williams, Kenny Anderson, Dennis Rodman, Scottie Pippen, Latrell Sprewell, and many many more from the NBA found themselves bankrupt and in debt once their careers are over. Pg. 208
http://sports.yahoo.com/nba/blog/ball_dont_lie/post/The-sad-tale-of-Ray-Williams-10-year-NBA-vet-no?urn=nba,253262

xli
University of Phoenix website http://www.phoenix.edu/ Pg. 215

xlii. Business Week statistical data http://www.businessweek.com/articles/2012-11-15/the-complete-2012-business-schools-ranking Pg. 215

xliii
2012 Business Schools ranking http://www.businessweek.com/articles/2012-11-15/the-complete-2012-business-schools-ranking Pg. 216

xliv
2012 Entrepreneurship Schools Ranking http://grad-schools.usnews.rankingsandreviews.com/best-graduate-schools/top-business-schools/entrepreneurship-rankings Pg. 216

xlv
Top 25 Graduate Programs for Entrepreneurship http://www.entrepreneur.com/slideshow/224419# Pg. 217

xlvi
Top 25 Undergraduate colleges: Pg. 218 http://www.entrepreneur.com/topcolleges/undergrad/0.html

xlvii
Rev. Hutcherson is part of the pastoral staff at Greater Love Tabernacle Church in Dorchester, MA 02124-1705. The overseer and founding pastor of that church is Pastor William Dickerson Pg. 223

xlviii Mr. P has asked that I conceal his real name to avoid being stigmatized. Pg. 223

xlix
Dwayne "Pete" Campbell was born on July 22, 1966 and died October 7, 2011. Pg. 224

l
I have a video clip on V4DV that you can watch of Nido Qubein asking the question, why do most immigrants become millionaires? It is a statistical fact that more immigrants come to this country and reach a level of success that most Americans never reach. http://archives.voices4thevoiceless.com Pg. 228

li
This training was given by Eric Worrie in New Jersey's International Airport Hotel. It was one of the best 12 hour training days I ever took part in. Pg. 231

lii
The tittle of the book is *The Big Idea* Pg. 232

liii
An interest book that you should read on the topic is *Immigrant, Inc.: Why Immigrant Entrepreneurs Are Driving the New Economy (and how they will save the American worker)* by Richard T. Herman and Robert L. Smith Pg. 233

liv. Alan Greenspan served on the Federal Reserve Board from 1987 – 2006 and was quoted on CSPAN-3 on 12/17/09 making this statement. His hearing was re-aired on 12/29/09 Pg. 234

lv Diagram is based on my opinion and observation of economic prowess. Pg. 235

lvi To learn more about Walther Reuther's contribution to American history, you must read *While America Aged* by Roger Lowenstein. Pg. 239

lvii CBS news headline: "Study shows 1 in 7 New US Marriages is Interracial"- 2008 Pg. 258
http://www.cbsnews.com/stories/2010/06/04/national/main65 47886.shtml

lviii
Book by George C. Fraser Pg. 259

Selected poems featured in this book can be found in *Pages from My Heart*. You can purchase a copy online as an Ebook or paperback on Amazon.com. Please note that the Ebook version does not contain any illustrations. You can also order an autograph copy by going to http://poeticimageryinmotion.com

27879745R00171

Made in the USA
Charleston, SC
24 March 2014